I0760712

Publish Her Anthology

BETTER TOGETHER

A Collection of Essays on Women Gathering

PUBLISH HER ANTHOLOGY: BETTER TOGETHER

ISBN: 978-1-962457-00-2 (Hardcover)

Printed in the United States of America
First Printing: 2023

Published by Publish Her, LLC
310 1/2 Main Street South
Stillwater, Minnesota 55082
www.publishherpress.com

Edited by Anna Befort and Chris Olsen

Cover art by Kprecia Ambers

"We are each other's harvest;
we are each other's business;
we are each other's magnitude and bond."
—Gwendolyn Brooks

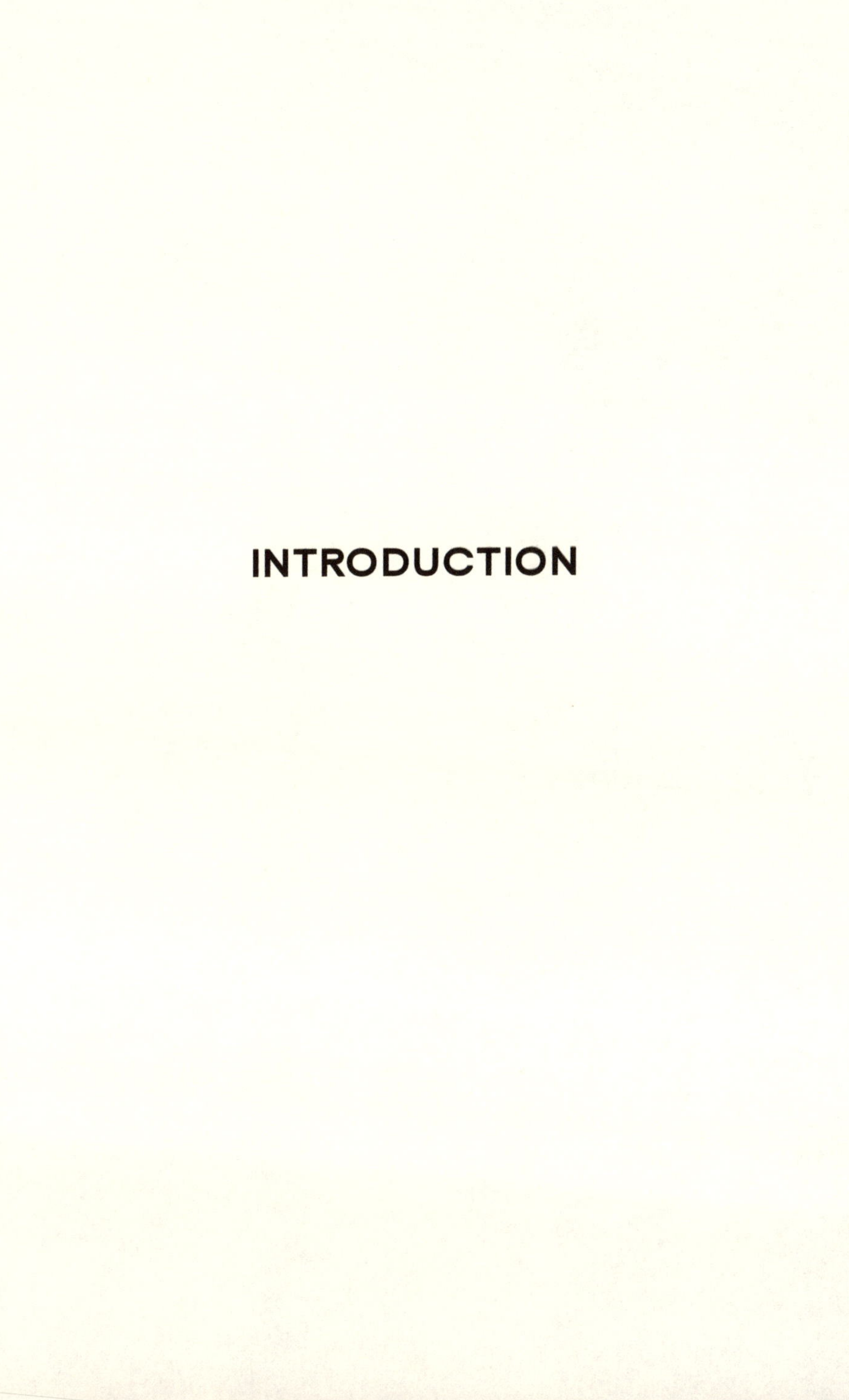

INTRODUCTION

Thank you for your support of this Publish Her anthology, "Better Together." This book is a celebration of women and relationships and so much more. It demonstrates the power of women joining together to make a difference in the lives of others. In addition to sharing their heartfelt stories within these pages, as a collective, the authors are helping provide access to women who may not otherwise have the opportunity to publish their work. By reading and sharing this book, you are contributing to these efforts as well.

Many authors dream of signing a book deal with a traditional publisher and making it to the top of the New York Times bestseller list. But only around 1 percent of authors are published by traditional publishers, which equates to fewer than 8,000 people annually.

The majority of authors published traditionally are white men ages 40 and older; these men are also at the top of the publishing pay scale. Meanwhile, the odds are stacked against women authors. Even more so if she is a woman of color, a woman with a disability, a member of the LGBTQ+ community or any combination of these.

Publish Her is on a mission to disrupt that status quo. We are a female-founded publisher dedicated to elevating the words, writing and stories of women. We are passionate about amplifying the voices of women of color, women with disabilities and members of the LGBTQ+ community, and we aim to make publishing an attainable, exciting and collaborative process for all. We want every woman to know: Your words are worthy. Your voice is important.

Publish Her demonstrates its commitment to equity, in part, by providing access to publishing services and programs through grants. One hundred percent of the proceeds from the sale of this book will benefit publishing grants for underrepresented women authors. For information about our publishing services and program grants, visit www.publishherpress.com/grants.

THE BUOYANT MOMS CLUB

By Cindy Lehew-Nehrbass

My hands, palms cupped like fins, push the warm water of the hospital therapy pool—out and in, out and in—pretending to scull myself afloat. Meanwhile, my memories revisit my former university's rec center pool, where a friend first taught me how to dolphin dive backward (one giant arc from the surface to the drain and back up) with a single breath. Once, in preschool, I'd tried to do a somersault in a neighbor's shallow pool but spent way too long twisted and stuck underwater before resurfacing, breathless. Afraid for nearly 20 years, I didn't attempt that feat again until I found myself coerced into a college synchronized swim club where I conquered my fear of drowning via underwater tricks with my eyes wide-open in foggy goggles.

Now my armpits stretch lazily over a thick black inner tube—the kind my husband and I rent to journey down the Apple River, hooting as we catapult over its mini waterfalls and boulders. But this moment is relaxing, almost Zen. And, as I bob in the incidental waves made by the other pregnant moms flutter kicking nearest me, all I can think of is wanting to slide out of my tube and practice a back tuck, oyster move or waterwheel.

This therapy floating session is far from my college days, when we were dealing with chilly water, fancy hair buns, skull caps and nose clamps. I am in a new club this time, and boy are we a sight. Our hair is chlorine-stringy, our bellies big with babies—

some carrying multiples, or most (like me) carrying very sick infants. Our swollen legs dangle beneath us, weightless. I am one of a half-dozen bed-resting baby incubators: gestating moms wheeled down ramps into the water by physical therapists, inner tubes slid over our chests, floating contently into the deepest end. We look like a swim team in our matching black nylon suits. Most of the swimsuits are stretched to the max, except mine, which is baggy and hangs like drapery over my waist, since my child is underweight. My daughter loves swimming in my uterus, supported by the hydrostatic pressure of the pool's viscosity cradling my abdomen, which lifts all stress from my pelvic cavity.

I've done this ritual twice daily for over six weeks to help generate more fluid in my amniotic sac and increase blood flow to my daughter's faulty heart. It also gives me a chance to be upright and reciprocate support with others in my predicament. My hospital roommate floats to settle a jittery uterus carrying twins; another woman suspends herself in the water to keep one of her triplets from squishing its siblings. Occasionally my mom and sister join me, sitting on the bleachers, their presence cheering me on toward another weekly milestone: my personal "gold medal" for the successful growth of my baby. But most of the time it is just me and the other moms hovering over our children and talking about the lonely days, sleepless nights, tasteless food, rounding specialists, new prognoses and dreamed outcomes.

When someone goes missing for a day or more, the rest of us process what it might mean: healthy babes born or, if too early, grieving families. For most of us, we know we will probably meet again in the NICU with the other moms of preemies, babies with heart disorders and ones that just can't thrive. We call ourselves the Buoyant Moms Club, and we are all high-risk moms—the ones nurses and doctors fret over. We will never give birth in our hospital rooms; we will never take our babies home right after a typical post-birth stay. We will not have what moms whose babies are not in the NICU—who stay in their homes, go to work and live outside the walls of this place—have.

I remember, when I was in the synchronized swim club, we trained together in camaraderie: a group of young women trying to match each other in strength and flexibility. We lifted weights every day and took ballet barre classes to perfect our port de bras so that we could execute beautiful "blossoms" with our arms in synchronicity and rhythmical cannons. We practiced our feet extensions so hard we'd get calf cramps, but our leg lines matched like a fine flock of flamingos. By the time I stopped training, just before competition season started, I was learning to mirror my friend in the crane position, sculling upside down, facing each other. But I never learned how to do a lift or how to push my teammates to the surface, though I'd always wanted the strength to do that. And I was never petite enough to be a flyer who gets thrown out of the water like a porpoise at play.

My Buoyant Moms Club jokes every now and again about my synchronized swim and dance experience (I'm a choreographer) and how we could try to make formations in our inner tubes and freak out the hospital staff. Yet our sessions are spontaneous improvisations, not choreographed water ballets.

We float close together in loose circles, tube to tube, whispering in hushed voices of our fears for our unborn and their unknown futures, supporting each other with calm words and arm touches. A support far superior to the liquid molecules shifting beneath our buoyancy.

Then one of us—usually me—will start sculling circles, slowly rotating the tube until the rest join in. On those days, we giggle, or at least smile, and I can see the faces of these women as they might have looked before pregnancy trauma changed their lives. I marvel at how under the water's surface we match perfectly in our egg-beater treading and how we have the grace of an Olympic team. I almost expect some inspirational song to play over a loudspeaker. Then, the physical therapists call us back to the wall and assist us onto our wheelchairs, wrapping us in towel blankets. We nod goodbye to each other, with arms tucked round our babies, and silently hope we all make "practice" the next day in our personal quests for our motherhood gold medals.

CADILLAC CAMPERS

By Kathie O'Brien

It's 1984. A women's softball team bursts into a dive bar in a small town in western Oregon. They're carrying a huge trophy. Single women in their 30s, boisterous, bursting with excitement, oozing confidence and joy, they dance as if they own the place.

Shouting to be heard over the '80s rock music, a bar patron manages to ask, "Did you win?" The team roars with raucous laughter and hands him the trophy. He reads the inscription out loud. "McGoo's Tavern 1984 Women's Softball … Beer Drinking Champions." The team erupts, high-fiving each other proudly.

Partying ensues and, eventually, the women decide they can't bear to have this magical evening end. Eschewing life's responsibilities, they throw camping gear into cars and drive the winding road to the coast. One of those foolish 30-somethings is me.

That night, the Cadillac Campers are born. It's a tradition that endures—a gathering at the end of each summer to celebrate life, share stories, enjoy each other and play.

The first year, we camp at a secluded place by a lake, set up a dozen tents with twice as many coolers, and spend the weekend. The only rules are no men, no kids and no pets.

In the years that follow, we fully embrace our status as Cadillac Campers. We certainly do not rough it. Fancy drinks, gourmet food, a plethora of blow-up floaties, and many, many comfort items are requirements for the weekend. Saturday is theme night. Themes vary: prom night, black and white, orange and black, tacky, Western, Hawaiian. They're different every year but always full of camaraderie and joy.

As we get older and are less inclined to sleep on the ground, camping loses its appeal. Our disposable income increases, and we discover condos and then vacation rental houses.

Over the years, we experience love and loss, marriage and divorce, children born and miscarried, illness and injuries. Some women move away, and some stay. Through the years, one thing is constant: The Cadillac Campers gather every summer to share stories, commiserate, celebrate, play and make extraordinary memories. So many memories. The time when a loved one secretly dropped a sailboat at our campsite and we sailed all weekend. The time when we hiked to the top of a mountain to enjoy a spectacular sunrise. The time when we watched dozens of whales play in the bay. The time when a bat swooped around a bedroom (suffice it to say there was much shrieking and waving of pillows—and laughter). That incredible week at the Pendleton Roundup. The list goes on.

Twenty years pass in the blink of an eye. One of the group members composes a song. We sing it every year now. Badly. We don't care. We sing and enjoy every minute:

"We've howled at the moon at night, hiked to greet the dawn ... Sunshine, laughter, food and drink, some tears and nonstop chatter ... A weekend with the CCers, it just don't get no better ... What would life be without the Cadillac Campers? ... Not for the faint of heart, you gotta be strong ... But you're gonna have fun with the Cadillac Campers ... The wild and wonderful Cadillac Campers!"

In each of our families, "Cadillac Camper" is a household phrase, an integral part of our lives, our sanity, our identity. Significant others know these few days together are non-negotiable. The relationships are unbreakable.

These are women we can count on to be there when life throws a curveball. Need someone to pick up some paint for you? We're there. Need someone to help your husband unpack because your moving date got screwed up and you have to be out of town for work? We're there. Need someone to hold your hand and listen to the horror of a loved one with a serious illness? We're there.

We've stayed in tents, condos, beach houses, glorious homes, modest cabins and even a houseboat. Every year has been unique, remarkable and oh-so-special. The 40th anniversary is just around the corner. We've slowed down a bit since 1984, but wherever we go, the celebration will include love, support, sharing, playing and fun.

When we meet up, our eyes still see those wild youngsters of 1984; age has not changed us. Our skin is still smooth, our hair is still lustrous, our bodies are still lithe, and our muscles are still strong. However, we are aware that we now look at most of our lives in the rearview mirror. We understand that in the not-too-distant future, we will face the loss of a beloved Cadillac Camper. We ask ourselves, "When will the first of us go? How will it happen?" Nothing can prepare us for that eventuality, the empty chair at the table, the empty drink glass, the empty bed. But we will go on; we'll be there for each other. After all, "Cadillac Campers, Cadillac Campers! What would life be without the Cadillac Campers? Not for the faint of heart, you gotta be strong!"

The Cadillac Campers may not solve any of the world's overwhelming social issues, but that's OK. It's enough for us to get this opportunity to truly be ourselves. Our daughters and other women in our lives have grown up knowing firsthand how important it is to have healthy female friendships. We watch as they too enjoy strong, supportive friends who gather regularly, and we revel in the fact that we have helped them see how important it is to build encouraging, supportive female bonds. These relationships are not to be underestimated or taken lightly. They are to be treasured.

Our influence will carry on long after the last of us is gone. My daughter refers to all of the Cadillac Campers as her "godmothers." She tells me she hears our voices whispering words of wisdom as she navigates adulthood. I know she hears, "Be strong, respect and take care of the women in your life, take time out for yourself, and have fun."

CIRCLES

By Kris Woll

"Dear Friend,
I felt it shelter to speak with you."
—Emily Dickinson (in a letter to
Thomas Wentworth Higginson)

Both of us were, that year, far from home. That was not a secret to anyone. She was named after where she was born. Meanwhile, someone from my office—my first real job, in an arts center—told me I appeared "corn-fed." (This wasn't nice. Also, I had to look up what it meant.) But there we were, one Southerner and one Midwesterner, living in adjacent apartments—brick, boring, square apartments—on the only street in that entire valley without a lovely view of the New England hills.

She moved there for graduate school. I followed love. We found each other in a Tuesday evening graduate class on the dusty sixth floor of a brutalist building on the edge of a big campus. She complimented my shoes after our first class, shoes I had purchased the day prior in a secondhand store off the idyllic main drag of the town where we were both living. The secondhand shop was just steps from the cemetery where our favorite poet (we would learn this about each other in subsequent conversations, but also, it was a widely shared sentiment in the area) rested under a mossy gravestone. The poet had once been a homesick woman herself, though she was living much closer to her home than either of us was. The poet returned to her family manse after a brief time just over one set of hills and never again left it. She gardened, tended to her family, looked out her window, and wrote and wrote and wrote—wrote even about mossy gravestones.

Sometimes life seems to be a series of circles.

When my friend and I met in the sticky warmth of early autumn in the valley of those historied hills, we were studying the past—a history course had brought us together. We were, in that year, somewhere between where we came from and where we would go. The whole thing now seems a metaphor.

We were friends for a year. Our friendship moved quickly. From shoe compliments, we suddenly began sharing clothes. We read novels together—novels not assigned in our shared class or her graduate program, most often set in my Midwest or her South. We discussed them on long walks and over coffee. We talked endlessly about where we were from. We cooked and ate and compared notes on food from back home—my tater tot hot dish, her grits. We took in the New England-ness around us with interest, joined together in our outsiderness.

The year moved full circle, and I cried and cried the day my friend moved, off to her first real job on the other side of her graduate degree and many states away. Before she pulled out of our shared parking lot on the street without a view, she handed me two bags of her old clothes and an armful of used books and her new phone number, as this was in the days when numbers didn't follow us. We said we'd keep in touch and visit, but we rarely did the former and have never, not in all these years, done the latter.

And with that, our friendship became a beautiful little history.

My friend kept me afloat in a particularly uprooted year. I was young and unmoored, and while I had been very enthusiastic about the adventure and romance of moving to a new poetic place, I hadn't really thought through all the ordinariness that awaited on the other side of that move—the sinus infections, the bills to pay, the car maintenance, the day job full of mail merges and changing printer toner, the petty and not-so-petty arguments with an equally young partner, the long and quiet afternoons that follow leaving most everything you know behind. I was lonely when I met her but much less lonely after I did.

This was decades ago now, a truth that is humbling to acknowledge. In those intervening years, we both moved around. We became mothers. We had careers with twists and turns, but they've gone in the general direction we plotted over coffee back in that valley. We both found our way, our winding way, back somewhere near where we started.

Circles, again.

And so, this isn't a story of a friendship that has lasted for years and years, at least in the way we think of "lasted"—full of shared experiences and regular contact and intertwined lives on the same path. But it is a story of an important friendship, one of my most important, even if the very close days were brief. We were friends in a very tender moment, in a specific time and place, and we had fun and laughed and learned and explored and shared secrets and sadnesses in those quiet whisper voices you use for secrets and sadnesses, and we had the same taste in shoes, and she accepted me—lost, young, uncertain, a bit too romantic me—just as I was. She made a difference in my life that year, and in so doing, she made a lasting difference in my whole life.

Just because something is brief doesn't mean it doesn't matter. Warm and funny memories from those days often come back to me and make me smile. A distant friendship, perhaps, but one I return to with gratitude in my heart.

Circles.

I adore her still.

CONNECTED

By Anne Pinkerton

It's 6 o'clock on Thursday evening—almost any Thursday evening—and I have a date. A date with my two long-term besties, Karen and Jena. A standing date we've held firm, with rare exception, for more than three years—ever since COVID-19 made us feel so alone. It's hard to imagine ever spending Thursdays with anyone else now.

I pour myself a drink. Maybe it's red wine, maybe a gin and tonic or a beer, depending on the season and my whim. I get comfortable on the couch in my living room, set my laptop on the coffee table, fire it up, and click "start" on a big blue button. If my friends are running late, I practice guitar until faces appear on screen. Jena, with her dark eyes and brunette bangs, is usually framed by the brick-red wall in her kitchen. Karen is either in her plant room surrounded by branching greenery or in her living room with her golden retriever nestled beside her. Once both of them appear, we officially begin.

"Hi!"

"Hi, honey!"

"How was your week?"

Virtual cocktail hour wasn't our creation, of course. When the pandemic hit, loads of people connected this way for months, maybe even a couple of years. But I don't know anyone else who has kept it up the way we have. Others seem to have disengaged over time, but most people in our lives know not to ask us to hang out on Thursdays anymore. I continue to have a standing weekly "meeting" in my Zoom work account for Jena, Karen and me. Naturally, it's my favorite meeting and the one I am most delighted to host.

Everyone is sick of online meetings by now, starving to see each other in real life, even for business purposes. The three of us are no exception—that would be our preference—and yet here we are. The technology has not only kept us engaged when there was no alternative, but it's meant that Karen and I are able to see Jena every week, even though she lives nearly 2,000 miles away from us. When she first moved to Texas several years ago, away from us in western Massachusetts, it was nearly impossible to imagine a way to stay as close as we are now. We have our computers and apps to thank. Weirdly, we also have an airborne, highly contagious illness to thank. Because otherwise we might not have explored this option.

Now we get a window into Jena's sunny backyard or pretty kitchen once a week. We compliment her cats, who wave their tails across the camera, and she talks to my corgis, who bend their heads wondering where the voice is coming from. Karen shows us her new furniture, plants or artwork. If the weather is cooperative, I sometimes sit on my wraparound porch, and they see my lush green side yard. I take screenshots instead of selfies to mark these moments.

In early 2020, when we first started, I used to attend our gatherings from a room upstairs, away from my then-husband, who would be watching TV downstairs. Seeing Jena and Karen on screen was a portal to relief and joy, into the faces of beloved women and away from both the terrifying state of the world and the stress of feeling jailed in my decaying marriage.

Since then, I've divorced. Both of them were there to figuratively hold my hand through the entire process, and I don't know how I would have managed otherwise. Now Jena and I compare notes on online dating (it's terrible, no surprise), and Karen has gotten separated. We have commiserated about our romantic lives, cheered each other, listened hard and sometimes cried.

The three of us have stayed up with the developments in each other's work lives, too—the triumphs and the pain points. We talk about mutual friends, what we learn in therapy, how to navigate tricky family issues. Sometimes our Thursdays are like parties. Others are more somber, depending on what's happening. Just like any regular get-together with the people who know you best.

Karen lives only 15 minutes away from me, and—now that the worst of the crisis seems behind us—we sometimes get together at one another's house at 6 o'clock on Thursdays so at least the two of us can be in person. Together, we peer through the glass at Jena, as if into a fishbowl, wishing she was with us.

We are all in each other's physical presence when we travel to either Texas or Massachusetts to see each other, but it's never as often as we would be if we all still lived close by. So Thursdays remain sacred. Occasionally, one of us has a personal or work conflict now. It always miffs us all, as if the world at large should recognize the inviolability of this ritual. But we adjust. We move our visit to a different night or have a longer session when we're back on schedule.

As the evenings draw out, the light of the setting sun filters through mini-blinds, painting stripes across Jena's face. We watch the sky turn aquamarine at dusk behind Karen. I turn on more lights in my living room, the glow of lamps illuminating my face, warmed by our sisterhood week after week, month after month, year after year. This abiding company of women is as real as anything—nothing virtual about it.

CONNECTING THROUGH THE OUTDOORS

By Wendy Altschuler

My one-woman shelter was staked near dozens of others in a tent city in the mountains of northwestern California, sandwiched between two lakes. Inside my warm lilac sleeping bag, which was cinched tight over my head, I blinked at the sole strand of lights illuminating my little haven. A proper night's sleep was imperative because tomorrow would bring big adventures, bright and early, and I'd need my strength and resolve.

For a single weekend, I would join a team of strangers, all women, and gain a deeper understanding of multiple outdoor sports, utilizing the newest and most innovative gear to hit the market. First up: a day hike to practice outdoor navigating skills. I often get turned around with a weak sense of direction, which is an occupational hazard for a travel writer. While I am no stranger to hiking and backpacking—they're two of my favorite things to do—I was interested in not only strengthening my map and compass reading proficiencies, but also connecting with other women who were doing the same.

There's something about sweating and working my body in the outdoors that bonds me to others. I find it freeing to discover that difficult times, like laboring uphill with weight on my back, never last forever. The awe-inspiring and blissful moments, like reaching the peak and enjoying a hard-earned snack, also don't linger indefinitely. It reminds me that when things go awry in life and I feel like I've hit rock bottom—don't fret, the clouds will part, the rain will stop, and the sun will shine again. It also reminds me that when I'm on a high, ecstatic like nothing can touch me, this feeling too shall pass. Gratitude is cultivated when I can really appreciate sitting with the middle bits where, for most of us, real life steadfastly happens.

Learning how to rock climb with a professional ice and rock climber from an outdoor women's collective was on the agenda next. The group was a mixture of females ranging in abilities. A couple ladies had no experience with outdoor rock climbing and had never been to an indoor climbing gym; a few, like me, had been climbing once or twice; and a few others were solid outdoorswomen who just wanted to get out and touch some rock. We set forth on a short hike, with our backpacks full of gear, and squeezed our feet in climbing shoes just before attaching ourselves to the ropes. The fear of those new to the activity was visible on their faces at first. But you know what? The support of the women in the group was all they needed to motivate them to give it their best. To try.

Providing an inclusive environment with the singular goal of exposing women to something new in the outdoors made the day's adventure incredibly inspiring. Without this supportive community, cheering everyone on and celebrating each other's successes, it can be intimidating or downright debilitating to try something new.

Feeling proud of myself, I signed up for a night run that was billed as easy for beginners. The pace started off at a strong clip, and my heart rate quickly increased before we even reached the hill. I wanted to push myself, yet I was panting and finding it difficult to get a full breath. I couldn't carry a conversation. Was it the altitude? Was I out of shape? Was this run too much to add after a day of rock climbing? Not even halfway through the run, I had to pull back. I was doubled over trying to catch my breath, panicked tears stinging my eyes. Through labored wheezes, which felt like I was breathing through a crushed straw, I told the group to carry on and just meet me back at camp. I didn't want to hold anyone up, and I felt embarrassed that my fitness wasn't on par. The women circled around me, and they all decided to walk with me until I could catch my breath. With the encouragement from new friends, we eventually made it back to camp, all together in one pack.

I learned from this experience that running, or doing something new and demanding, can make us feel vulnerable and uncomfortable. But it's this vulnerability that forces us to be honest and authentic, and that attracts meaningful relationships with others.

Later, around the campfire, a woman spoke about how she had lost her ability to reliably access her short-term memory. She was a professional runner and thought her career would be over due to her mental health. What she learned, however, is that her drive to push herself never dried up, and while she had some new cognitive challenges to contend with, she knew she had to find a way to continue doing what ignited her passion. Now she coaches others and inspires people to push themselves past what they think they're capable of. We are stronger than we think.

My body felt achy and sore as I inched into my tent that night. I knew I'd sleep like a ton of bricks. An old cowboy saying is that if you can't sleep well outside or if you toss and turn throughout the night, then you weren't tired enough.

The next day, I'd go kayaking in a foldable lightweight kayak and mountain biking on a single track before experiencing a final outdoor dinner with everyone at the camp. The tables would be covered with flowers in Mason jars, fairy lights would be strung overhead, and there would be a musician singing and strumming an acoustic guitar. Women would be gathered around picnic tables, buzzing about their weekend adventures. Some would exclaim how they couldn't wait to go climbing, hiking, kayaking, biking or camping again. They'd vow to make more time for themselves in nature, where fresh air, verdant landscapes and the night sky shows off. This is the power and magic of the outdoors. This is the power and magic of women.

COOKING WITH FIRE

By Katie Hanus

Six years ago, I invited several open, curious, and kind friends, all women who I knew would humor my interests, to gather with the purpose of honoring tradition, ancestors, community and food by cooking a meal together fireside. Many of them knew one another, but some didn't, and none of them had ever before been to my home.

I found myself worrying about the tiny detail that I didn't actually know how to cook with fire. Barbecue was traditionally a role left to the men in my family. They would stand together for hours near the grill, drinking beer, talking, laughing and smoking. By evening we all would enjoy the fruits of their labor—usually a brisket so tender it seemed to melt in your mouth. After making peace with the fact that my own lack of experience correlated strongly with the likelihood that the upcoming meal might ultimately not taste very good, I put my faith solely in the value of the shared experience and sent out email invitations.

Resisting many urges to try menus in advance to ensure our success, I revealed to my friends upon their arrival that, for better or worse, we were going to experiment blindly and figure this cooking with fire thing out together.

I prepared by purchasing skewers, coal, a small grill, a variety of raw vegetables, chicken, herbs, seasonings and sangria fixings, and everyone who attended brought something to share. The small grill I planned to use alongside my fire pit was still in the box when my friends arrived. When we started looking through the assembly manual and became discouraged by the extent of screws, washers, vents and handles not yet attached, it was tempting to pass the project off to my husband, thus allowing us to relax and visit until he brought it back. But I was surrounded by intelligent, stubborn, resourceful and determined women that day, one in particular named Christine, who would never concede to handing our experience over to a man.

Christine built the grill with the support of a few others, while I sliced raw meat into skewer-sized pieces and chatted with my friend Margaret. Others prepped vegetables and sipped water and sangria while visiting on our shaded porch.

When the grill and fire pit were lit, we let the coals smolder awhile before building our individual kebabs of meat and vegetables. Everyone got as creative as they wanted—some put slices of lemon and lime on their skewer, others put mango and pineapple among mushrooms and Brussels sprouts, and some added medjool dates as adventurous accessories to their chicken and onion along with a variety of seasonings and avocado oil. We each made our kebabs distinct so they would be easily recognizable when they came off the grill.

We had vegetable and fruit kebabs going on the fire pit and the raw meat kebabs on the grill Christine had assembled. As the meat and veggies began to sizzle, we chatted about Michael Pollan's Netflix series "Cooked," which we all had intentionally watched in advance. We noticed a red-shouldered hawk above us and doves cooing around us. When all was ready, we moved to gather around the table.

Karen and Alisa saw that we would now be sitting in full sun because of the hour of day, and they immediately took it upon themselves to move my porch table into a small slice of shade.

The eight of us managed to squeeze around the table and chatted about things ranging from the ethical decisions involved in raising and sourcing animals for food, to the different cultures and communities explored in the "Cooked" series, to our past jobs, to our kids, to random facts about health and nutrition, to silly stories about trying to outsmart squirrels who robbed bird feeders. We shared past experiences and excitement for upcoming adventures—one of us was moving to another country that same week—and other everyday moments of life, in the way women have done over meals for generations.

I was self-conscious as the hostess, worried about the stacks of clutter that surrounded my home and wondering if I should be guiding the conversation to topics I had initially wanted to discuss that we hadn't gotten around to yet. After time passed, though, I noticed what unfolded in its place. Probably not much different than the content our mothers and grandmothers shared with women in their own kitchens: stories about life and families, laughter and the future. Everyone's contributions were received and acknowledged with encouraging words and kind smiles.

There was nothing overly profound about any of our conversations that day, and some women ended up sharing more than others. We laughed—one laugh in particular was big enough to bring tears to my eyes, and I continued laughing for a few days afterward each time I remembered it. My favorite flavors that day were the grilled fruits: warm mango, date and pineapple slices paired with cold and creamy goat cheese. I also enjoyed the sprouted quinoa salad my friend Alisa shared with us.

The meal wasn't a culinary masterpiece of any sort. It was no longer hot by the time it was served, the meat was a bit tough, and we never actually made it to the s'mores. But it was fun. We learned a few things about cooking with fire and each other. It was community. And, maybe most important, it was ours.

DISCOVERING SISTERHOOD IN BOUJAD

By Mónica Lindo

I'd made Algerian friends during my term at University of Paris, so it was my first-choice destination for traveling in North Africa. However, that became impossible when it began experiencing civil unrest. It felt safer to visit one of its more stable neighbors. That's how I ended up in Morocco. Instead of backpacking, like I had done around Europe, I decided to go as a volunteer. Joining an international work camp would allow me to experience the culture while donating my time in service.

I signed up for a three-week project in Mohammedia, a west coast city between Casablanca and Rabat. There were 30 volunteers—21 local and nine international (from France, Germany, Japan and the U.S.). There was a main boulevard going through the city with palm trees planted in the median at about every 5 meters. Our job was to clean all the trash that motorists and passersby had thrown in between the trees, till the soil, and plant flowers on a 1-kilometer stretch of that road. Because temperatures regularly passed 40 degrees Celsius, we only worked until lunch time. Then we had the afternoons to explore the city, relax or visit a nearby beach. At the community center where we slept, we took turns preparing meals and cleaning. Some evenings we had impromptu parties in which we danced, drummed and sang to music from a dusty boom box.

During the last week of our volunteering stint, some of us

talked about doing a bit of traveling before leaving the country. My new Japanese friend Makoto and I decided to team up and travel for 10 days. Driss, a local volunteer, invited himself on our trip with the excuse that he could guide us since we spoke no Arabic. Then Abdel also decided to come along, but only until we arrived at Boujad, his hometown.

Makoto and I had expected to take buses or trains and stay at hostels, but Driss and Abdel had other ideas. They phoned friends or acquaintances around the country and asked to stay a few nights. This worked because hospitality is of utmost importance in Islam. The prophet Mohammed encouraged his followers to be good hosts and to receive visitors and strangers with kindness and generosity. That also meant that the itinerary was out of Makoto's and my hands. We made stops in Fez, Errachidia, Boujad and Marrakesh. All were cities where we knew people. In Marrakesh (which was the only city Makoto and I got to choose), we stayed at a friend of a friend's home.

It was also decided that we would hire a taxi to drive us for the first part of the trip. It had no air conditioning. Each time we arrived at a new home for the night, my main focus was to bathe. By the time we arrived at the third city, I was so done with riding in the sweltering back seat with these three boys who were competing to see who could go the longest without showering. To top it off, my period began, which heightened my sense of smell. More than ever, I needed to feel clean. Thankfully, I usually got a window seat, so I stretched my neck out the window, gulping fresh air to keep from retching at the stench of unwashed bodies in this ridiculous Stinkfest.

When we got to Boujad, Abdel's older brother and friend formally greeted us outside the family home and then again inside. We sat on red carpeting and leaned on red sofas within reach of low wooden tables. Women silently served us the customary sweet, mint-infused black tea along with flat loaves of bread to tear and dip in saucers of ripe olives swimming in oil. I put on my best face, followed whatever conversation was in French, and tried not to look too out of it when it switched to Arabic. I was sweaty, crampy, and desperately wanting to feel soap and water on my skin.

After a half-hour or so, one of the women came and discretely pulled me away. Four of Abdel's sisters were there. I was tickled to learn that two of them were named Latifah and Kadijah, like the hip-hop Queen and the character she played on the 1990s sitcom "Living Single." We sat in a little circle on the spotless floor near the kitchen. It was rare for them to meet and talk to a foreigner. Two had never finished school, so they only spoke Arabic. The two who did speak French translated for them. They asked about my road trip. "You poor thing, stuck with those brutes," one said. Another sister exclaimed, "Stay with us! No need to return to the living room."

I marveled at the decorative trim down the fronts and on the cuffs of their djellabahs. It turned out that they had hand-embroidered it themselves! They brought out a couple of garments to show me their ornate handiwork. Assuming that American women didn't do crafts at all, they were surprised to hear I crocheted.

One sister was a married teacher and mother of one. I'd

just finished my first year of teaching, and we bonded over our common occupation. Then another sister asked the sweetest question: "Do you want to shower?" I felt such gratefulness, I could've just hugged and kissed her. It was as if she'd offered me a gift of great value. She knew exactly what a woman traveling the dusty roads squeezed into a hot car full of reeking bodies needed. After a shower and change of clothes, I felt decent again.

That night, I fell asleep filled with gratitude, wrapped in the warmth of unexpected, newfound sisterhood.

EMBRACING THE DOWNWARD SLOPE

By Joy Riggs

Kathy hands me the sled. We stand at the top of a hill next to the Minneapolis house we are renting for the weekend with seven of our closest friends from high school. The night before, we toasted our collective 50th birthdays with sparkling wine and fancy mango cake. Today we are sledding. That's how we roll.

I grasp the flimsy foam rubber sled by a duct-taped handle. It's a loaner. Although I didn't bring my own sled, I have come prepared; I'm wearing nearly new fuchsia snow pants I bought two years earlier when I was under the mistaken impression I was taking up snowshoeing. I'm also wearing Canadian-made fake-fur-topped boots, purchased under the correct belief that comfort is more important than fashion when you were born the year the Big Mac was invented.

When was the last time I went sledding? I conjure an image of standing in my backyard at age 5. I am wearing a bulky zip-up-the-front "snowmobile suit." A steep incline leads from our porch down to the rocky shoreline of the lake. Mom must have planted our rectangular plastic sled in the snow and coaxed my brother and me to climb in with her. I don't remember the ride down. I only remember the view from the top. The anticipation of flight. The suspension of before and after.

I sit astride the borrowed sled and prepare to launch my 50-year-old self down the unfamiliar slope, which features jumps designed to enhance the experience. My friends and I are sharing the hill with a few parents and their elementary school-age kids, as well as a cute young couple who could be high schoolers or 20-somethings. From my perch, I spot some of my bundled-up friends tromping back up the side of the hill, out of the path of the sledders. They apparently survived their own runs down. This gives me hope.

I do not have any memories of sledding with my own three kids. It's one of my parenting regrets. When they were old enough to sled on their own, I sent them into our backyard, where nature and additional landscaping had created a perfect sledding hill—enough of an incline to offer excitement, but not so much that I needed to monitor their every move. In the event of excess momentum, the worst that could have happened was a soft, tangled landing in the lilac bushes at the edge of our yard.

I did not own snow pants in those days. Keeping the kids in snow pants that fit, locating matching pairs of mittens, and rounding up stray boots and hats sapped my energy for outdoor play. I reveled in the chance to stay inside where it was quiet. But after I cajoled the kids outside and before I turned milk, cocoa powder, and white sugar into the promised homemade hot chocolate—an improvement upon the packets of Swiss Miss and mini marshmallows of my youth—I'd linger at the back door and watch as Louisa in her hot pink parka, Sebastian in royal blue, and Elias in lime green took turns with the plastic saucers, the Radio Flyer toboggan, and the cheap snowboards. Pink-cheeked, joyful, quarrels forgotten, the siblings romped in the frozen wonderland, united by the rush of shared adventure.

The scene of them in our backyard plays in my head like it was yesterday. But it wasn't. Two of them are in college, and the youngest doesn't need snow pants for high school. And I am 50, on the downslope toward 100.

I dig my heels into the snow and push off toward a slippery path worn by those who came before me. Within seconds, the sled turns 180 degrees. I am facing backward. The sled is moving too fast for me to turn it around; I am at its mercy. I don't see the first bump, but I feel the jolt. As it propels me into the air, my stomach drops and I shriek. I land with a thud and barely catch my breath before I hit the next bump. Tears stream from my eyes, and I giggle the rest of the way down, while trying desperately not to pee my pants.

As I fly, I am not 50, I am not 5, I'm not a mom, a wife, a daughter or a friend. I'm a creature in fuchsia snow pants, kicking up a spray of powder, headed toward a future I can't predict with a wide smile on my face, trusting I'm headed in the right direction.

(This essay originally appeared in the Dec. 25, 2018, issue of the StarTribune.)

THE FIRST WEDNESDAY MORNING

By Amanda Kennedy

There were eight of us. We sat in a small room in an even smaller circle made up of a couple beige love seats and a few stackable chairs, brought in and unstacked. We hugged decorative throw pillows to our chests like shields or compression to a wound. Maybe both. The soft natural light coming in from the generous window was kind to our 30-something, 40-something and 50-something faces.

When my therapist suggested I try group therapy, I recoiled. She spoke of support and connection while I was smiling and nodding and writing it off. I was raised to suck it up and never complain, a practice I was steadfast in, but it wasn't working. While I'd recently given in to talk therapy as necessary medicine for my declining mental health, group therapy felt like a bitching and moaning club for bitter women. I certainly didn't want to participate in enabling a group of bleeding hearts, nor risk becoming one of them.

Underneath my resistance, however, was fear. One-on-one therapy was hard enough. Being in control was something I prized, so losing it in front of a qualified professional whom I paid $200 an hour was bitter medicine. Inviting eight or nine strangers to witness me breaking down sounded mortifying. Group therapy, I was sure, was not for me.

But to appease my therapist, I agreed to try it. "Try it"

meaning to go once or twice, never say a word, and then declare it not my thing.

When I arrived, I buckled down on my plan. I stayed mute but for my brief introduction, delivered with a tight smile. For my benefit, they took turns introducing themselves. These women had been meeting for long enough to know each other's ex-husbands' names, how many children they all had, and every facet of each other's relationships with their respective mothers. Context was established. As the new person, I had been briefed that I wouldn't be forced to say anything, but that my sharing would build trust among the group, something I wasn't concerned with because I wasn't planning on staying.

As the women came in and settled, they began talking among themselves. I checked the clock and saw we were five minutes in. When were we going to start? Were we waiting for someone? What was the agenda, I wondered? Diane, the therapist running the group, sat among us in the circle and rarely spoke, only asking a clarifying question here and there. After 12 minutes of chitchat, it dawned on me that the chitchat was the meeting. They passed a box of tissues while they opened up about their hard stuff, their easy stuff, their everything stuff. One woman spoke of the verbal abuse she was taking from her spouse of 18 years who flip-flopped between begging to try again and calling her selfish in front of their kids for wanting a divorce. She struggled to speak through her sobs while she relayed the scene at school drop-off that week when her 9-year-old wiped his boogers in her hair and said he hated her. She had managed to stay calm enough in the moment to tell him that she still loved him no matter what and then cried all the way to work.

I grabbed a tissue.

There seemed to be no time limit for how long each woman took to speak over the two-hour meeting. Some women shared brief highlights of what was going on in their lives, others simply offered encouragement and love, while a few others had heavy issues to unload in the circle. They took all the time they needed, and no one offered advice or solutions. No one said, “I’m so sorry,” “Why don’t you …” or “It’ll be OK.” It was clear that some things wouldn’t ever be OK, and that was OK.

Some women, like me, didn’t speak at all.

However, even in my silence I couldn’t help my tears from falling with theirs. Each woman’s pain poured out of them, inviting my pain out to mingle in their collective stew of hopelessness, depression, shame, trauma and grief. Though the sources of our suffering were different, we reflected it back to each other in our shining eyes, brimming and spilling over. I witnessed connection, authenticity and belonging—things I thought I knew but now realized I hadn’t felt until then.

It was overwhelming. The tight lid I kept on my pain came loose, and I was only a little bit embarrassed that I quietly cried for much of the two hours. Without a word or a look, the women made sure I always had a fresh tissue. When I occasionally lifted my eyes and found someone else’s, I saw love and knowing. Pain recognizes pain.

The two hours passed faster than I expected. Diane smoothed her hands up and down her thighs and looked up at the clock with a gentle smile. She looked around the room like a proud mother. "Thank you all for showing up and holding space for one another. When we stand in truth, we allow others permission to do the same. The armor we wear was not put on all at once, but piece by piece, hurt after hurt." She looked around the room at each of us, and my eyes met hers. "It will not come off all at once," she continued, "but piece by piece. When we bear witness to each other's pain, we validate their reality. We learn to trust others to do the same for us."

We slowly stood and gathered our purses and used tissues. We put the pillows back in place. I endured some awkward smiles and shoulder squeezes, but I felt no judgment for keeping quiet, only acceptance. There was a shift back into the reality of school pickup, grocery shopping and small talk among the women as we filed out into the hallway. I felt exhausted but also a little bit lighter.

Like I'd shed some armor I no longer needed.

HAPPIEST BABIES ON THE BLOCK

By Lindsey Rose

I was born into a loving family of anxious people-pleasers with control-freak tendencies. I swore I wouldn't pass these traits on to our two children. But in early January of 2007, when our oldest son, Ari, was 6 weeks old and not sleeping unless my husband danced with him to "Ain't No Mountain High Enough" blaring from the stereo, my sleep-deprived, postpartum being yearned for our new family member to start pleasing us with longer stretches of shut-eye.

I was dead tired, and back then there was no social media to keep me company through sleepless nights. My friend in Nashville already had a 12-month-old and was (and still is) my favorite source of parenting advice because she was always one step ahead of whatever stage we were in. She provided helpful tips in my moments of maternal cluelessness, and she recommended we watch "Happiest Baby on the Block," a video by renowned pediatrician and baby sleep expert Dr. Harvey Karp. His legendary "5 S's" are said to turn on your baby's calming reflexes and soothe the most colicky babies. I was ecstatic when she offered to ship her DVD copy to Minnesota.

Luckily, two of my lifelong girlfriends, Kim and Beth, were also on maternity leave with their newborns that winter. Since our days together at sleepaway camp, we'd dreamt of having babies close in age, and our wish came true. Our three children were born 18 days apart, a number that represents good luck in Judaism. My mother-in-law, Anita, whom Ari is named for, died unexpectedly three months to the day before he was born. I constantly looked for signs from her in the afterlife, and this village was one of them.

Motherhood was a magical new phase for our friendship—we held each other up when each of us needed it most, through the pain of sore nipples from our nursing baby barracudas and the triumphs of running errands without a screaming infant incident. We were there to help each other and didn't get caught up in comparing parenting styles.

During our maternity leave, we played musical houses, sharing the roses and thorns of new motherhood and keeping an eye on each other's babies so each of us could eat a bite of food or pee in peace.

I was so pumped for the pending arrival of "Happiest Baby on the Block" that I invited Kim and Beth over for a viewing party. They, too, were eager for advice to help achieve more sleep. The minute the video arrived, I emailed them because texting from my Motorola RAZR flip phone wasn't a thing yet. "IT'S HERE! WE'LL FINALLY LEARN THE SECRETS OF SWADDLING AND BETTER SLEEP," I announced.

A few days later, Kim and Beth arrived at our house with infants and nursing pillows in tow, and we ascended, boobs full, to the bedroom. The plan was to watch the DVD from bed and nurse the babes into post-feeding comas.

One of them held Ari while I strapped on my Breastfriend nursing pillow and popped in the video for our highly anticipated matinee showing of "Happiest Baby on the Block." I felt a sense of pride helping to provide parental education to my friends. I hit play on the remote, scooped up my sweet Ari and sat down alongside Kim, Beth and their infants to get comfy.

But as I looked up at the TV, I did not see Dr. Harvey Karp or any happy babies on the screen. What I saw were two adults having passionate sex over a pool table. Doggy style.

I gasped, stunned, and frantically hit stop on the remote. "WHAT ON EARTH? I swear this is 'Happiest Baby on the Block,'" I blurted. Kim and Beth shrieked with laughter, noting the scene was much juicier than the soothing "5 S's" promoted to them.

My husband and I had a dual DVD/VHS player, and I ejected the DVD to prove the label said "Happiest Baby on the Block." But when I reinserted it and pressed play again, there it was—a steamy show from the stars of the pool table sexcapade.

Had I just lured my nursing circle to our bedroom to watch porn? Maybe my Nashville friend sent this to me on purpose! Was she trying to remind me that I can't control everything? Was she trying to teach me how to spice up our nursing circle?

I felt paralyzed by embarrassment, despite being in the company of my closest friends. Kim suggested I try switching the remote from VHS to DVD. Sensing I was at a loss, Beth grabbed the remote from me to eject the VHS. But the DVD popped out AGAIN with a giant image of a smiley, blue-eyed baby next to a "No. 1 Parent's Choice" endorsement on the cover.

Finally, after more toggling with the remote, a prehistoric VHS popped out with a provocative film title. It was my husband's pornography tape that I later learned had been in there for a while—I was oblivious.

After we collected ourselves and stopped laughing, we fixed the tech glitch and were off to the races with Dr. Harvey Karp and his baby-soothing tips, which were ultimately quite helpful. I'm not giving any spoilers; you'll have to watch it yourself to learn more about the "5 S's."

"My friends and I learned a LOT from watching 'Happiest Baby on the Block' today," I said to my husband when he returned home from work. "You'll have to watch it with me later!" When he realized what had happened, he was mortified. Then we had the first of many chuckles over what is now known by our friends as "the legendary nursing incident."

More than 16 years later, Kim, Beth and I remain extremely close, as do our children, despite the X-rated content they witnessed as infants. And all three of them and their mothers are champion sleepers.

HOUSE ON THE LAKE

By J.J. McGawn

My body tingles with anticipation as I run up the concrete steps of my aunt's house in Minneapolis, Minnesota. The front steps are shaded by established elm trees, and I hear the whiz of bikes riding by on the lake path behind us. Aunt Tukie opens the front door before we reach it. Her brown hair is cut short, and she wears a short-sleeved collared shirt and long Bermuda khaki shorts. She bends down to wrap my siblings and me in a big hug. Tukie greets my parents and ushers us into the front hall. The grand living room sits to our left with parquet floors and gorgeous views of the lake. To our right, an ornate wooden banister soars up to the second floor.

Like a heavy moon, a big picture window hangs on the stairwell. Above it lies a smaller stained-glass window that was boarded up for years. After my aunt and uncle bought the house, they restored the home from top to bottom. In the process, they wrenched wooden paneling off the stairwell, revealing the elegant stained-glass window beneath. The window was so delicate that parts of it cracked during the jackhammering and heaving construction. Now, sunlight dances through the restored window, dropping purple and green light on the stairs.

Usually, my mother has a way of breathing down my neck, then icing me out with the flip of a switch. But at her older sister's house, my mother magically turns into a more docile creature. Immediately drawn to her sister, my mother asks how my cousins are doing, what activities they are enjoying, how they are doing with their friends. Her banter with my aunt floats up the stairwell.

My cousin Kate calls my sister and me upstairs to her room. We run up the staircase, past my cousin Chris' room with his model airplanes hanging from the ceiling. A beautiful porch with ornate spindles on the railing sits off Kate's room. There, we practice our summer camp dance routines as Billy Joel's "Only the Good Die Young" plays from the stereo.

Changed into my bathing suit, I walk softly downstairs and through the kitchen. My mother is engaged with her sister planning dinner. "What flowers should we use as a centerpiece? Do we have enough ice?" she asks. Relieved that they are busy, I scoot past the kitchen island and out the back door.

My brother races off the diving board and into the pool. Chris yells, "Race to the drain!" Eyeing the bottom of the deep end, I drop my towel on the ground, then run and dive into the water. Smoke billows from the grill on the patio. Nearby my grandmother sits in one of the folding chairs, soaking up the sun in her plaid pants and collared shirt. Her vodka tonic sweats in her hand.

After dinner, I hear adults talk in the kitchen as they finish the dishes. Aunt Tukie wanders into the living room and joins me on the couch. Out the front window, the sun is just starting to set, sending rays of pink light across the lake. The grand piano my great-grandmother played to entertain guests at her lavish parties sits on the side of the room. A pile of my self-published, handwritten books sits beside me.

"Let's read one together," Aunt Tukie says, picking up "The Lonely Swan." It is one of my favorites. When I wrote it in second grade, I knew the adults would think that I was the lonely swan, so I deftly named her after my sister.

"Why did the swan need to go outside of her pond to make friends?" Tukie asks.

"She played better with the ducks. It took her a while, but once she found them, she was happy," I explain.

"I see." Aunt Tukie nods knowingly behind her thick glasses. She pats my bare arm.

"Tukie!" My mother's voice is raised, anxiously looking for her sister.

"We're in here," Tukie responds, giving me a smile.

My mother walks around the corner from the kitchen into the living room and sees us sitting on the couch. She stops dead and stares. My eyes immediately go to my lap.

"We are meeting Sally and Bill for drinks," my mother says to Tukie, her jacket in her hand.

Then she turns to me. "The sitter will be here to watch you and the other kids. Now go upstairs and get ready for bed, please." I look up at Tukie, sad that our time together has come to an end. She smiles and gives me a wink. With that reassurance, I feel a bit lighter as I climb off the couch and head upstairs to find my pajamas.

* * *

My mother's cousin, Aunt Kitty, is in her late 80s, almost the same age Tukie would be if she were still alive. Aunt Kitty looks fabulous with her gray hair in a bouffant, pulled back with a plain brown headband. "The trick to looking young, girls, is to keep the same hairstyle," Aunt Kitty advises.

We eat frozen custard in Kitty's car after a drive around the lake, and she tells me that she was "very close" to her Aunt Janie, my grandmother. "My own mother wasn't a warm fuzzy," Kitty explains with a smile as she scoops up her vanilla custard. "But your grandmother took the time to listen and gave great advice. When I had a problem, she was the one I went to." My jaw goes slack, and I almost drop the custard. I loved my grandmother dearly, but she kept an emotional distance. I can't imagine her as a confidant.

Then it strikes me: If Aunt Kitty didn't connect well with her mother but found solace and support in her aunt, maybe I still could too. Even though Aunt Tukie died decades ago, it still feels as if she is rooting for me. I think Aunt Tukie knew I was the lonely swan after all, and at her house, I found my duck.

LIGHT BEARERS

By Heidi Fettig Parton

Late in the summer of 1989, at the start of my sophomore year of college, I saw the new film "Dead Poets Society." A few days later, I changed my major from visual arts to English.

Never before or since have I possessed such clarity of vision.

The movie opens with a scene set in the intimate stone chapel of Welton, a private New England prep school for boys. Parents and expectant students gather, the boys clad in dark blazers, their hair trimmed neatly in styles of the late 1950s. Bagpipes begin to play. A stooped white-haired gentleman, bearing a lit candle, guides a procession into the chapel. He's followed by some older students holding up banners embellished with words like "tradition" and "excellence."

During the ceremony that follows, Welton students are introduced to Mr. John Keating, a relatively young new English teacher. Later scenes bring us into inspirational teaching moments, with Mr. Keating employing novel ways to teach classics from Shakespeare and Walt Whitman. I left the film whispering the Latin phrase "carpe diem." Seize the day.

In high school, I had revered John Hughes' films, such as "The Breakfast Club" and "Pretty in Pink." Although these films taught me to embrace my unique quirks (I believe I was the only student wearing their dead grandmother's clothing to school), they didn't cause me to hunger for knowledge like "Dead Poets Society" did.

I grew up in a small town in northern Minnesota. My parents, both public school teachers, struggled to pay the mortgage on a modest three-bedroom ranch home. Private school was not an option for me. Yet, although my secondary school years didn't supply a teacher quite like Mr. Keating, my public school district did attract a string of outstanding English teachers. All but one of these teachers between seventh and 12th grade were women, and these English teachers were beacons in that frigid prairie town.

But I didn't recognize that at the time.

I wouldn't recognize it until I'd spent nearly two decades in law, as a lawyer and then in legal publishing, before clawing my way back to literary writing. As I began to write and publish my own essays, four of these former English teachers of mine became "friends" on Facebook. They read my words and encouraged me with their comments; they invited me to call them by their first names. I was their peer now, and their aging faces didn't seem that far off from my own. How young they must have been when I was their student.

It turns out that Ida, Sharon, Judy and Jan weren't all that different from Mr. Keating. How could I have been so impacted by "Dead Poets Society" if my love of literature had not already been primed by these women?

Reflecting back, I see the flickers of light.

When I was in the seventh grade, blond-haired Ida sowed my fascination with Greek myths and archetypal characters. Ida also possessed a biting sense of humor that still comes through in her politically left-leaning Facebook posts—especially invigorating during the Trump years (which, unfortunately, we haven't really emerged from).

A year later, in the fall of 1983, Sharon became the first person I ever called Ms. (Ms. Knowlton). From Sharon, I learned that a female didn't have to announce her marital status to the world. It was also in her class that I read Anne Frank's diary entries for the first time. This small but mighty book showed me the power of true, honest words, and it was my gateway to a lifelong love of the kind of nonfiction that's now called creative nonfiction, the kind of writing that provides the container for my own heartfelt scrawls.

When I was a sophomore in high school, Judy introduced me to Harper Lee's "To Kill a Mockingbird." She also became my coach when I joined the speech team a year later. Dressed in smart tweed jackets, she brought out the best in our team of misfits. With Judy's guidance, I discovered that "drama" was my thing when she handed me a scene from Bertolt Brecht's "The Jewish Wife" to memorize.

That final year, when I was so ready to be done with school, Jan assigned George Orwell's "1984," three years after the actual 1984 and 30 years before the book's themes would ring eerily similar to real life.

Kind but firm, Jan also required her seniors to keep a journal. I still have that spiral notebook, the cover decorated with a black-and-white magazine photo of a goth-looking teen walking across a lonesome prairie. These journal's entries hold clues to the pervasive dread that hung over me that year. In one of Jan's notes, written with a green felt-tip pen in the margins of my journal, she empathized with me: "Oh Heidi. High school doesn't hold much for people with your intelligence and talent." In another, she encouraged me: "Your journal is a joy to read, Heidi—thoughtful, reflective thinking and feeling." Her last comment was a request: "Heidi, I hope you let me know what you're doing in 10 years."

Jan couldn't have fathomed the emergence of Facebook back then. Neither could Judy, Sharon or Ida. None of us knew that one day they'd read my words again, that they'd be "connected" to me, these surrogate mothers, these guides.

At the end of the procession that opens "Dead Poets Society," the older gentleman, the candle bearer, lights one of the youngest boy's candles, and from there, the "light of knowledge" is passed from student to student, brightening the dimly lit chapel.

If I squint my eyes and look to the north, I can see myself, a solitary high school student walking across a stark, frozen prairie. I thought I was alone, but now I see them flanking me: Ida, Sharon, Judy and Jan.

MELINDA

By Sarah Schellenberg

I was a preschool room mom once. I didn't want to be. During the years my three children were in preschool, I had always been the mom at the top of every room mom's shit list, so I was shocked when they asked if I would like the "honor" of being room mom for the class of 4-year-olds known as the "Four Day 4s." The other moms reminded me it was my last child's last year of preschool. That was all it took. I caved. But I'm glad I did. That is a truth I often forget: Sometimes, the thing I least want to do is the first step to something I was meant to do.

A week later, I dropped my daughter off at her classroom and headed to the basement where I, the room mom, would run a meeting for her classmate's parents. That's where I first met Melinda.

She was sitting in the back corner with my friend Margaret. She had dark blonde hair and bright blue eyes, and she was dressed better than most of us. As I spoke to the other moms about sign-up sheets and silent auctions, I noticed this woman's shoulders bobbing with laughter. She and Margaret were having fun, and I was pissed. Not because they weren't paying attention, but because I wasn't in on the joke.

As was customary, each parent introduced themselves and talked about their child. It was the new mom's turn.

"Hi, my name is Melinda, I'm an alco … oh wait … am I in

the wrong basement?" Half the room erupted with laughter—the fun half.

Melinda had just moved to Connecticut from New York with her husband, Jesse, and their two kids, Ellie and Cole. After the meeting I approached her and Margaret.

"Margaret, please tell me, what was so funny? For a second, I thought my fly was down."

"Christ, Sarah. We all know you don't own pants that button, let alone zip."

With my chin up, I proudly declared, "Damn right. I'm wearing maternity pants and my youngest is 4." I looked at Melinda and extended my hand. "Welcome to Wilton. I love your jacket."

"Thank you! I like it too! You might wanna get used to it. I'll try to trick you bitches into thinking I'm not wearing the same thing four days in a row by throwing on a scarf or changing up my earrings. But don't be fooled, I will funk this shit up before Halloween."

Hmm, I thought. If I catch her braless at drop-off, I may have found a soulmate.

Over the next few months Melinda wasn't around much. Working in Manhattan as an art buyer, she usually wasn't at pick-up where the chatting happened. Meanwhile, the rest of the moms started to bond. Family playdates were made. A group was forming. On the rare occasion Melinda was there, she would buzz in, make everyone laugh and buzz back out. I liked her. Everyone did.

There are some things I know to be true. I know the quickest way to get a man to exit a conversation is to mention a tampon. I also know the things that change you the most are never planned. They slap you in the face on a random Tuesday when you thought all you had to do was buy salt for the water softener.

It was a Tuesday in January when Margaret approached me at drop-off and said we needed to talk.

"Melinda is sick—really sick." She took a deep breath, and it caught in her throat. A face that usually sparked with mischief looked scared and tired. "Cancer. Bad cancer."

"Shit." It was all I could say.

Between parents and friends being diagnosed, cancer seemed almost contagious once I reached my 40s. But this was nothing like my father's slow-growing prostate cancer. This was bad cancer. Melinda had been diagnosed with triple-negative breast cancer, and her tumor was growing fast.

"We have to do something," Margaret said.

"Of course," I agreed.

That day I embraced my role as room mom and began sending emails to rally the moms of the Four Day 4s. Melinda barely knew us, but she needed us. We would make her life easier by dropping off meals or her children after school. We never expected her to invite us in. Through Melinda I learned a new truth: In the darkest hours, if you choose to keep the door open, there will be light.

Melinda quit her job, started chemo and had a mastectomy. She went to every soccer practice and recital. She celebrated the first day of kindergarten with the other moms at a coffee shop. She belly laughed with us, despite having found out days before that the cancer had spread to her liver. She decorated her home. She rescued a dog and called him Motherfucker. She lived.

In December, Melinda floated around her house in a bathrobe elegantly passing out pancakes to 5-year-olds in pajamas. Without a hair on her head, she was more beautiful than in any of the pre-cancer photos on her wall. We all sang "Happy Birthday" to her daughter and marveled at Melinda.

She died almost a year to the day Margaret enlisted the help of our mom group. Six weeks after Ellie's birthday celebration. She died at home surrounded by family a few hours after some of us had gotten into bed with her, held her hand and prayed. After we promised those babies of hers would always have a bunch of batshit crazy ladies looking out for them.

It has been eight years, and I still marvel at Melinda. I will always be grateful for the time and friendship she gave us. When she let us in and let us love her, she gave us a chance to see not just her goodness, but each other's as well. We are all still friends. Still laughing and still opening our doors to each other when we need a little light.

OLDIES

By Kathleen English Cadmus

We gather around a rectangular table in the dining room of the home of my friend Kathy. A recent widow, she lives here with her daughter and son-in-law. Watching her talk about the past year and her husband's death, my eyes stray over her shoulder to the view outside. I watch the calmness of the pond, the perfectly placed trees, and the serenity of the crisp winter night as she speaks of the ambiguous loss during her husband's dementia, the pain of losing him, and her days now peppered with unrest.

We first gathered together decades ago as young nurses and childbirth educators. We embraced Lamaze, a birthing movement in the '70s sometimes referred to as "natural childbirth." Lamaze was associated with feminism and a concern for the whole person—a preparation for childbirth that promoted education and relaxation in lieu of heavy anesthesia and physician-controlled deliveries. The idea to form our own Lamaze education group was conceived in the modest living room of my Cape Cod-style home. I remember feeling the flutters and tiny pulses of quickening of my third son. It was the winter of 1974. Our evening ended late. Thoughts swirled through our heads about how we would empower women to make informed decisions about their birth experiences. We pondered what to call our dynamic group, born from camaraderie, liberal convictions and defiance. Morning brought a call from Ruthie proclaiming our name: LCA, for Lamaze Childbirth Association.

Over the decades, there were more than 30 of us who taught for LCA, but the increase in technology and acceptance of epidural anesthesia during labor eventually altered the focus of childbirth education. As fewer community classes were needed and childbirth education moved into the hospitals, LCA was no longer in business. About a dozen of us wanted to stay connected, so we continued to gather, nameless, in each other's homes. During spring break, a few of us flew to visit Elaine in Florida. Elaine picked us up in a van with a sign announcing "Oldies." The name stuck.

* * *

There are six of us Oldies around the table tonight. Next to Kathy sits MaryBeth, my best friend since the beginning of my time as a nurse; she's the only one in the universe who can make me laugh at myself and life, even in moments of irreverence. Beside me is Sue, my first Lamaze instructor and the person who is most responsible for getting me into this scene. Sue is the most unconditionally accepting person I have ever known. Ruthie, our organizer and the one with the most class and dignity, sits at the opposite end of the table. Serene Eileen, who taught us nurses how to teach with grace, is the last in our group to have qualified for AARP.

It is December 2022. Tonight is our first holiday get-together since December 2019. We are the science believers, the medical protectors, the overly educated hand washers and the mask-wearing preachers. We come together tonight as the COVID-19 vaccinated, boosted and negatively tested. Pat, who was one of this city's first to volunteer for the COVID vaccine, is absent tonight because her husband is ill. So is Kathy G., whose table we sat around decades ago interviewing, deciding if they had the qualifying LCA strengths and passions. Dorothy, whose three babies match up with the ages of my three sons, is out of state with her daughter's family. Elaine, who christened us the Oldies and was the first to earn her doctorate, is at home in Florida. The most distressing absence I feel is Judy, a dynamic, funny and passionate soul who was our first education coordinator. She was the first to teach me how to teach. Judy died this past summer, yet she will never leave us.

My memories of first meeting Judy, christened Julia, are vivid. She came to my home in 1971 delivering teaching materials, six weeks into my orientation as a Lamaze instructor. Judy was seven years older than I and dressed in a free-flowing tie-dye dress and Birkenstock sandals. I was feeling contentedly like Mother Earth, my breasts pulsating from the milk building for the next feeding of my second son, the gold medallion from "Another Mother for Peace" resting in my nursing-induced cleavage. "War is not healthy for children and other living things," it declared in black script matching my long, dark hair. The strongest memory I have of Judy is in the hours and days after my son (the one I was nursing when we met) died suddenly at the age of 11. He was a blue-eyed, vibrant boy with a grin as wide as the canyon he fell into. Judy had words, wisdom, and kindness for my surviving two sons, lessening some of my burden of soothing their pain.

It is easy to see what brought us together. We were mothers, mothers who wanted freedom to fully express and manage our bodies and minds in childbirth. And we were nurses, educators with a passion to let others know about this power.

What brought us together has also sustained us, magnetically drawing us to gather for decades. We shared beliefs. We shared experiences. We taught others, and we taught each other. In the early years, as we gathered for business meetings, our babies and toddlers came too. We passed them around to each other to cuddle, hug and nurture—a gathering of our offspring at our center. We cared for each other during postpartum, provided meals, and helped during illnesses and emergencies; one woman even nursed another's infant during her hospitalization.

We cried together.

And we laughed together until we cried, bellies aching.

The Oldies were a need conceived and born within us, nurtured by gathering together.

That we've all been here in the same space at the same time, I call, like childbirth itself, a miracle.

OPEN TABLE

By Suzanne O'Brien

Steaming mugs of tea are clustered in the middle of the round wooden table. Four of us share paints, brushes and ideas on this snowy Saturday afternoon. Women with self-imposed to-do lists and the worry that our worlds would fall apart if we didn't touch everything in them. Unplugging for a few hours feels indulgent. We collectively shake off our discomfort. We need this time together.

My family rarely eats at this table, which has hosted so much more than meals for a century. Quartersawn oak. Simple pedestal. Clever, sturdy extension design that supports three additional leaves, transforming the table's circular shape into a generous oval. "That's why I bid on it," my grandmother once said of the table she bought at a sale barn auction for 25 cents. "So there's always room for anyone who needs company."

Lisa's phone chirps. She looks at the screen, takes off her glasses and turns away from the table to answer. The kettle rattles in the kitchen, and I slip out to refill our mugs. The conversation is brief. "I'm at Suz's now. I'll be home later," says my best friend of more than 30 years. There is tenderness and resolve in her voice. When she puts on her glasses and picks up the paintbrush, I can almost feel her exhalation.

The table came to my grandparents' farm kitchen, then to my parents' city duplex and then back to the farm again after my dad died. When I got married, Gram offered the table to me. She'd found another one. "Not as nice," she said of the linoleum-covered surface, "but it gives us plenty of space." I knew the "us" she was referring to. Grandpa had died years before, but that table still served as a gathering place for the many women in Gram's life, a community for practical and creative arts.

Sonja holds up a tube of Pyrrol scarlet paint and considers it, wrinkling her nose. "I think I'll add this orangey red." Her calm confidence serves her well as a pediatrician and mother to four boys.

"Do it," Richelle, now an art teacher, answers without hesitating. The two had bonded over a shared love of art during the coming apart of Sonja's marriage.

"Is that how you encourage your students?" Lisa teases.

"Pretty much." Richelle takes a sip of tea. "Except for a few eighth-grade girls. One of them called me a bitch last week."

Around Gram's table, I'd witnessed sewing circles and golf course anti-expansion meetings, canning sessions and quilting bees. Feathery indentations formed on my knees from the stitches of the chair pad as I'd begged to help my grandmother and her town friends peel buckets of windfall apples. Then there was the summer evening that I squeezed onto Gram's chair to join a rousing Scrabble game with a group of neighbor ladies. All of the women were widows, though that never occurred to me at the time. I was more focused on the bottle of 7Up and the dish of peanuts awarded to me for helping keep score.

After my first marriage ended, I brought the table to the home I live in now with my second husband and our daughter, just down the street from Lisa. When my mother moved in a few blocks away, we started a knitting group that grew bigger than the fully extended table could accommodate. A nearby coffee shop became our gathering spot, and we carried the spirit of the table with us. That same group of women brought their wool and needles and encircled my mother's hospice bed at the end of her life. I hoped Mom felt their love and heard their laughter as she was letting go.

My family finds errands to run so I can host afternoons like this one. A few hours of community, creative expression and presence. And sometimes gatherings happen spontaneously, like when my teenage daughter and her friend joined me around the table the previous weekend. One minute they were sprawled on the sofa looking at their phones and the next we were painting together and talking about crushes.

The only sound in the room now is the sigh of a pan flute. "This is so great," says Sonja. "So Zen."

I wonder aloud if it might be the spa playlist and lavender mist.

"No, it's just so great to be—" she trails off, looking down at her painting.

"—together." Lisa finishes the sentence.

"Cheers to that," says Richelle. "Can we come back next week?"

Soon Sonja pulls on her coat, and Richelle gathers up the mugs. Lisa packs away her paints and gives me a hug. We are reluctant to leave, but this afternoon together will nourish us until the next time.

Gazing at the empty table minutes after my friends leave, I realize the reason my grandmother made space for her friends wasn't really about the things they were creating or the problems they were solving. Those women didn't gather only to sew the quilts or to stop the timber from being swallowed up by a development company or to figure out how to live alone or to even finish a game of Scrabble. Just like we weren't together today merely to make art.

They sat around the table—we sit around the table—for each other. We show up and we hold each other up, for no reason at all or during the hardest of times. Gram's table symbolizes an enduring space of deep belonging that allows us to be, if only for a few fleeting hours, fully present, fully ourselves.

THE QUILT

By Deb DeBates

The sunny yellow quilt lies crumpled on an open futon that is set flush against a knotty pine wall in the loft of our lake home. A large black bear pelt hangs above, its head nearly touching the bedding. As I lift and spread the quilt, I admire its evergreen borders, the uniformity of the squares, the quality of the stitching. Kneeling on top of it, I tuck one side between the wall and the futon. My head bumps the bear's brown snout as I back off the quilt and replace the pillows and stuffed animals, arranging them just right.

Our 16-year-old son, Micah, sleeps here when we come to the lake. I don't remember telling him his grandma Jan made this quilt; he was just a baby when she gave it to our family. I haven't explained how she created it alongside the other women in her church quilting group. If I'd had that conversation—which I think I will soon—I would have explained that his grandmother was involved in many groups and organizations during her lifetime, not just the quilting group. There is so much he doesn't know, and I suppose so much I don't know either. I rarely asked my mother for details of these gatherings, or maybe I never asked at all.

What I do know is that on lazy weekend-at-the-lake mornings, when I come upstairs to make this bed, and when I handle this yellow quilt, my thoughts turn to her.

In the 1970s, my mother was a busy farm wife and mother of four young children, living just outside of a town of 2,000 people. Her life was consumed with family, household and farming responsibilities. But throughout that decade, there were evenings when she put on a nice dress or pantsuit and drove into town to attend a meeting of "Friendly Farmerettes" or "Homemakers Club." The names of these groups make me chuckle now, and I wonder what was on their agendas. I imagine they must have been a much-needed diversion for women who wanted a little female companionship and conversation.

In areas like the one I grew up in, church was where most found community. My mom could be found at "Ladies Aid" meetings on a certain weekday afternoon. My siblings and I would often ditch the school bus, dropping in just as the meeting was ending and they were about to have coffee and dessert. Mom never missed these gatherings, perhaps because she was often the president of the group. These women thrived on serving others, and they did so together for years. I imagine they felt a bit like sisters working on shared projects, which often included things like teaching Sunday school or hosting bake sales, which, at that time, seemed to lack male involvement. In later years, a few of these women and my mom became involved in the LWML (Lutheran Women's Missionary League), which required them to travel to a larger neighboring town for meetings.

The quilting group started when my mom was well into her 50s; its purpose was to help those less fortunate, including people in developing nations. In my mind's eye, I see her with her scissors in hand, cutting squares of fabric and stitching them together with her sewing machine. I picture the other women, once very familiar to me, working diligently alongside her in the fellowship hall, fabric spread out on tables, the chatter of their voices mixed with the whir of sewing machines. I see their faces, sometimes serious with concentration and other times smiling and laughing.

Oh, how I wish I could go back in time and mingle among them. What would they talk about? Or would they work together in comfortable silence, having known each other for so long, like family? Would they lift each other up, encourage one another as they carried out their creative endeavors? Would they cut and sew and quilt for a couple of hours or longer? Did the work make them happy, energize them, bring them a sense of satisfaction that remained throughout the day?

When I look at this quilt and smooth my hands over it, I feel like part of my mother is still with me. Wrapped around the melancholy that has been there as long as she's been gone is the inspiration the quilt provides. It reminds me that serving others was a big part of who she was; it was what connected her with other women and, ultimately, greatly enriched her life.

It was an example that now greatly enriches my own.

THE REQUEST

By Jody Vallee Smith

I had been asking the universe for a group of women who desired lives integrated with purpose and impact. Days spent volunteering at my daughters' elementary school were making me weary. I learned that small talk leaves me exhausted. I was seeking relationships based in deep connection and a belief that the world could be a better place. I was determined to do my part and wanted to do so alongside some extraordinary women.

I found those women when I signed up for a group called Mother's Quest. The only obstacle was meeting on something called Zoom. I was unfamiliar with the platform and tended to bumble when it came to technology.

In a couple clicks, I saw myself in a grid on my screen and thought of "The Brady Bunch" opening credits. I hummed the theme song in my head while we waited for everyone to arrive. When all of us were present, introductions ensued.

Cristin lived in Astoria, New York. She worked in higher education, had a podcast and was raising one son. Her background in theater production was obvious from her animated personality, her aptitude for possibility and her vernacular. She seemed powerful and the kind of woman who would tell the truth.

Katie lived in Austin, Texas. She was studying herbalism and home-schooling her two daughters. By the end of the Zoom call I could tell she had an abiding connection to nature, was a deep thinker and was longing for like-minded community. She also felt like a long-lost friend.

Nancy lived in Berkeley, California. She was a freelancer who did grant work, provided support to caregivers and was raising two adopted daughters living with chronic conditions. She used phrases like “grit and glitter” and looked for magic constantly. She seemed sparkly and wise.

Julie, the facilitator of the circle, also lived in the Bay Area. She founded Mother’s Quest while raising her two sons. Like the rest of us, she feared she was losing herself in motherhood, so she reconnected to her voice and her longing to make an impact outside her family. She was dripping with purpose.

After a two-hour Zoom call that included a meditation focused on the future and a reflection circle, we decided to keep in touch via Voxer, a walkie-talkie app where we could leave messages around our different schedules and time zones. Another technological hurdle I would have to push through. We started our daily check-ins on Voxer for accountability, but it evolved into what has become, for me, daily medicine.

As our circle of five began to find a rhythm, the breadth of our discussions expanded. We spoke of parenting challenges almost daily, and as time progressed, we shared health diagnoses of family members, the passing of parents, the building of businesses and our never-ending search for meaning in it all. We held each other’s virtual hands through enormous amounts of grief. We held each other’s virtual hearts in the moments when parenting seemed impossible. We celebrated small personal victories and big business milestones. Our circle was navigating life together, and we were all better for it.

Then in March of 2020, the World Health Organization declared a global pandemic and, soon after, George Floyd was murdered. Interactions that were once joyful were now filled with anger and terror. Fear cloaked every voice memo. Between our parents and children, we had many medically complex individuals among us. Simultaneously, as a group of women who considered ourselves allies to Black communities, it suddenly didn't feel like enough. We were steadfast in trying to convert allyship into activism. But the slog of the pandemic made everything feel impossible.

Cristin needed to escape New York City. She lived across the street from a hospital and was traumatized from the incessant sirens and people dying. Her job seemed futile, and her inner entrepreneur was getting louder. So when the opportunity arose, she moved upstate and started a consulting company. She now helps people reorient their relationship to work, establish personal worth and create soul-fulfilling lives.

Katie blogged about suburban homesteading, went through death doula school and launched a small herbal business. Tending to her land calmed her nervous system, and being prepared for another catastrophe calmed her mind. She remains focused on providing historically accurate home-schooling curriculum for her girls. She recently moved back to her hometown to nurture the side of her that craves community.

Nancy, a white mom with two Black children, was doing her best to guide them through the racial divide ravaging our country. As she continued to bump up against systemic issues while navigating their health, she took her advocacy work to state and national levels. She is using her industry experience and her voice as a mother to reform the system for future patients.

Julie continued to find ways to move into activism. She took her sons to protests, actively supported political candidates and continued to have difficult conversations on her podcast. When life gets busy, she reminds herself of the importance of finding a path for authentic action. She continues to model for her children how to advocate for themselves and others.

I'm launching a company called Courageous Girl, a call to action for women and girls to create more intentional lives based on personal values, rather than "happily ever after." My days are spent rebelliously modeling enchantment before chores for my two teenage daughters.

This circle of women forces me to look beyond hope and into action. We are not only imagining the world we want to leave to our children, but we are co-creating it. It is happening in our homes, our communities and our Voxer channel. By witnessing each other's lives and sharing our experiences, we are healing together as women are intended to. Our circle is an all-encompassing, nonhierarchical representation of the wheel of life. On some days I am the student, on other days the teacher. But every day I am a mother, wife, sister, friend, businesswoman and someone who will continue to fight for a future I believe is possible. These women have been an integral part of my journey. I thank the universe every day for fulfilling my request.

SISTERHOOD

By Karol Jackowski

While I have found everlasting sisterhood with the Sisters for Christian Community, my life's path into sisterhood began long before I entered the convent. There is the family into which we are born, and there is the family we choose. I met the first sister I chose in my "family of friends" on my first day in kindergarten. Veronica is my lifelong best friend, and her son Joe is my godson. I have also kept in touch with six of my other school friends, always meeting at our high school hangout, House of Pizza. We meet for lunch and most often stay for dinner because we can't stop talking and laughing; we don't want our reunion to end. And after one of us departed this life way too soon, nothing changed. We still reserve a table for seven. They are the best and longest-lasting members of the family I chose, and these grade school and high school friends are especially fun to be with.

"Fun to be with" was also essential in the sisterhood my mother found with seven neighborhood women who called themselves "Chères Amies," or "Dear Friends" in French. They were mothers of kids who went to school together, making it feel as though I had eight mothers and another big family. They met monthly in each other's homes to smoke, snack, drink cocktails, and play pinochle or bunko. No kids or husbands allowed. I still remember sitting on the bottom step with my sister Jackie, often until after midnight, listening to the women howling with laughter and wondering what was so funny. There were also Chères Amies Christmas parties and summer picnics. They attended each other's family weddings, baptisms and funerals. Some became godmothers to each other's children; two of the Dear Friends' grandchildren even married each other.

My mother was the last surviving Chère Amie. I'm certain her Dear Friends were the first to welcome her Home, just as she envisioned. Those Dear Friends were the family she chose. Those Dear Friends turned us into one big family. My sisters and I were born and raised into the sisterhood of Dear Friends and wanted Dear Friends of our own. My sister Debbie found that as a Scrabblette with three other women, also moms whose kids went to school together. They meet monthly to sit around the table, drink cocktails, eat their favorite foods and play Scrabble. No husbands or kids allowed. They have helped raise each other's children (and grandchildren), celebrate holidays, mourn one another's losses and accompany each other to chemotherapy. And my sister Jackie is a Yaya with four women who meet regularly, also eating and drinking and celebrating. As for me, I found that kind of sisterhood the day I entered the convent.

On my first day in the convent, just like my first day in kindergarten, I found sisters who have remained dear friends. There are ties that bind sisters in a convent together in ways nothing else can. In vowing a simple life, a solitary life, and a life in community, we became soul sisters. There is powerful strength in numbers, and the sisterhood promises to bring joy into this world and grant peace on earth. That's the call I hear to sisterhood. When I entered the convent, I found a family of friends who are exceptionally fun to be with, the kind of sisters I wanted in the family I chose. There were six of us who met the first day and have kept in touch ever since. Four of us left the convent and got married; two are dearly departed but remain with us evermore. They are always somewhere in my mind and appear in my dreams. Even the sisters in the convent that I don't keep in touch with, those I haven't seen in decades, still feel like soul sisters whom I'd love to see anytime. My life found itself most at home with the Sisters for Christian Community in which we vowed to create sisterhood wherever we are.

After I left the convent and began teaching at a college, the women I worked and played with became part of the family I chose. I was a member of "The Secret Order of Judith," which consisted of seven colleagues who, like the biblical Judith, wanted the college president's head on a platter. We met on Friday nights, called each other "Judy," drank Manhattans, served extraordinary meals, unloaded our burdens and lifted each other up. And when we parted ways and scattered all over the country, we kept Judyism alive; some of us still meet annually for a week on the Oregon coast. I spent a day with a Judy one month before she departed this life. We planned how we'd keep in touch, promised to think of each other every day, and blood-sealed the deal, thumb to pierced thumb. Four of us gave a happy death to another Judy who was terrified of dying. On her last hospice day, we swabbed her mouth with Manhattans, told our funniest stories, and ate fried chicken, coleslaw and french fries—her favorite meal. We kept our promise that she would not die alone. The Secret Order of Judith remains forever in the family of sisters I chose.

I now live on the Lower East Side of Manhattan, where sisterhood becomes me. There is a group of four who call ourselves "The Marys" because of our devotion to the Mother of God, the Goddess. When we meet, we call each other "Mary," drink cocktails, and serve favorite foods and soul talk. Hearty laughs lift our spirits higher every time. We attended one woman's wedding and another's ordination. We prayed for one of us to have a baby and then baptized the child a year later. For "The Marys," communion doesn't get holier than that. I see myself now as a sister to everyone I meet. The greatest grace I've found since the day I set foot in the convent is how to find soul sisters wherever I am. Mission accomplished. Blessed be sisterhood.

THE SONG IN YOUR HEART

By Jane Ramseyer Miller

For our 50th birthdays, the four of us gathered in New Mexico for an extravagant celebration. I was in the middle of a 30-plus-day bleed and had left a painful marriage. I was exhausted and grateful to be held by these women who have supported me my entire life. We lounged in hot pools at a spa, cooked fabulous food, drank delicious wine and offered gifts to one another. My gift to each of the others was a mug with a collage of photos from our annual gatherings and this message:

"Friends are those people who know the song in your heart and sing it back to you when you have forgotten the words."

Not only do we know the song in each other's hearts, but we know each other's siblings, parents, schools, churches, boyfriends and girlfriends. I still know their childhood phone numbers. I could draw a floor plan of each of our family homes and tell you which bedroom belonged to whom.

We grew up in a Mennonite town in northern Indiana. Our parents were Mennonites. Our grandparents were Mennonites. We each had a parent who taught at a small Mennonite college, and that's where we met—the Goshen College Laboratory Kindergarten. It didn't feel like a laboratory, but it did have a large two-way mirror across one wall where faculty apparently observed students. I was oblivious, but Barb recalls crawling on top of the bookshelves and pressing her face to the mirror to see who was watching us inside the secret room.

Like a laboratory, growing up in a Mennonite community offered a sense of security and also persistent scrutiny. Along with a deep sense of belonging came pressure to conform and to make the "right" decisions as a child and young adult. Although our brand of Mennonite was left-leaning, coming out in my 20s was a painful experience. While Mennonites value peacemaking and nonviolence, they were not ready to embrace LGBTQ+ folks. While I was rejected by my church community, my childhood friends were unwavering in their support. We share a love that is beyond blood and truly unconditional.

Our annual gatherings began the summer we dispersed after college graduation. For the first decade, our gatherings involved tents in the woods, cooking on camp stoves and making annual "predictions." These elaborate conversations over a long weekend were recorded in copious notes and included an annually updated "marriage order"—the sequence in which each of us was predicted to be married—which was somehow crucially important to us in our 20s. We also listed what we thought the next year would bring for each of us as outlined in categories: home and city, work, spirituality, important people and major issues.

Decades of annual gathering notes are still stored in "the envelope." In examining the tattered envelope recently, I discovered that the annual predictions in our 20s were not only documented in writing but dutifully signed by each of us. I was, and still am, the keeper of the envelope, even as its contents have changed significantly over the years.

During one miraculous decade, the four of us randomly ended up in Minnesota. Coincidentally, Lori and I moved in the late '80s—she for grad school and I for a chance to live in community with a group of college friends. Barb arrived two years later for med school. Julia followed soon after to pursue a job in education. We intermittently shared apartments, cars, friends, meals, road trips—and always our annual gathering.

In our 30s, our annual gatherings involved "fingernails," a term that evolved from dedicated time each of us took sharing thumbnail sketches of our lives over the past year. By then we had transitioned to gathering in cabins and sleeping in beds, including a few times at a favorite Wisconsin farmhouse with several of our babies in tow. With age, we moved away from predictions, instead selecting an image and word that represented the past year.

At our 40th birthday gathering, my gift to the others was "The Divine Secrets of the Ya-Ya Sisterhood" by Rebecca Wells. We became known as "The Ya-Yas" to our spouses, our children and likely our therapists. It was during this decade that we realized we each needed a private room. And often, the first order of business was a long, solitary nap.

Together we have traversed breast cancer, marriage, divorce, betrayal, miscarriage, birth, a brain tumor, coming out, deaths of siblings and parents, joys and worries about our children, sexual harassment and years of therapy. And we have devoted hours and hours to singing.

Eventually Barb moved back to Indiana, and a decade ago the three of us in the Twin Cities began gathering every Monday morning for tea or a walk, occasionally bringing in Barb by Zoom.

In 2022 we celebrated our 60th birthdays at a spa in Wisconsin. Our annual sacred sister gatherings continue. As always, they include cooking, walking and singing. These days, we eat fewer brownies and more vegetables. Sometimes we share quiet moments gazing at the water or North Woods. But more often, the silence is filled with song. We have sung the songs of the Medical Mission Sisters, tunes from musicals, Mennonite hymns. We have rehearsed melodies for an upcoming wedding and joined our voices in deep harmony—the familiar four-part harmony from childhood that still lives in our blood.

THE SUM OF US

By the Cedar Ridge Writers Group

(Eileen Drennen, et al.)

At the same time every Friday, faces from New Jersey and Ohio, Boston and Canada, Minnesota, France and places in between join together on Zoom. With a press of a few buttons, we're sitting in the same video room, each of us beaming in from our own little square of planet Earth.

One by one, our faces appear for the gathering of the Cedar Ridge Writers group. Most meetings, we're six, eight, or 10 people, but we'll meet even if we're just two, three or four. We arrive from rustic kitchen tables and airy bedroom desks, book-lined studies and sunny front porches, an audio link in a car and even an RV in the desert.

We come from wherever we happen to be, and we come as we are—hair done or undone, full makeup or barefaced, in our work clothes or in garden togs and a black trucker hat with LOVE spelled out in white letters across the front.

Not knowing what or who we'll find is part of the fun. We don't always read each time—there are times we show up just to listen. Some days, we share tears and hold one another's grief as we relive a hard-edged childhood, share a cancer diagnosis on the page, or reassemble offline as an email brigade to send funds after a house fire. Other days, we tell stories on ourselves, letting it all hang out. Then we catch one another's laughter as easily as the international virus that first brought us all together for a week in January 2021 at an online writing workshop.

The writing intensive about craft and publishing attracted multiple screenfuls of faces, and its rapid pace made it hard to connect with our fellow writers, some of whom already had memoirs or novels underway, others of whom dreamed of creating longer works but hadn't yet figured out how.

None of us wanted those days of writing, sharing and learning to end. Just in time, Ryder Wyatt offered to start a writers group for anyone who wanted to keep the fires burning. We added our names to the chat, collected emails and RSVP'd. Her vision was centered on meeting weekly and reading our work aloud.

Ryder christened us the Cedar Ridge Writers, after her family's heritage farm and a workshop series she'd founded, but she didn't tell us at first that the grace of her invitation would work both ways. We were giddy she'd lit a path for us to follow, eager to see what might happen if we committed to showing up for ourselves and one another. She was grateful to learn she wasn't the only one struggling with loss or divorce or death—or even writing—and trying to find words for what still felt too hot to touch.

We met one another across tiny windowpanes: the glamorous woman who lived in Paris and just finished a novel; the soft-spoken teacher whose first drafts sounded like finished pieces; the poet who lived in Minnesota and carved odes to ice with her sharp details; the youthful writer whose descriptions of lakefront life put sand between our toes. We were daughters and sisters and aunts, mothers and grandmothers who found the right words in one another's company.

Week after week, as we read aloud our stories of wonder, joy, heartbreak and mystery, our voices grew stronger—in our bodies and on the page. Those of us who started out uncertain we could even call ourselves "writers" began trusting the group enough to show the raggedy edges, no longer afraid to be fully present, tell difficult truths and bear witness. We lifted one another up and urged each other onward. We evolved as peers and leaders. We listened to one another's voices break as we read a challenging passage; we read through tears and ended up feeling free.

A few of us have gotten the chance to meet in person, and we felt as if we climbed out of our tiny windows into real relationships and hugs. Still, on Fridays, we extend our virtual arms around each other's shoulders as we remind ourselves of who we really are and who writing is helping us become. We celebrate one another's publications—an essay, a poem, a book! Together, we grow braver. Grateful members of a trusted sisterhood, we gift one another with time and attention; we listen with our whole hearts.

Like the gold used in the Japanese art of Kintsugi, our writing group has made disparate parts into a new and stronger vessel. We may always be distant in geography, but we are intimate witnesses to one another's most profound stories.

At the same time every Friday—wherever we happen to be.

THE TROPICAL CURE

By Krista Westendorp

The lemony scent wafted our way. A curtain between us and first class hid the midsection of the flight attendant handing out small, steaming white bowls and cloths to passengers before lunch was served. My friend B.J. tugged on my arm: "I want one of those!"

"We're in coach. We can't have them." She looked faux devastated.

"But I REALLY want one."

"You could ask the flight attendant. The worst that happens, she says 'no,'" I suggested.

"Excuse me!" B.J. spoke urgently. The flight attendant turned a kind face to her. "Do you think I could get one of those little bowls they have up there?" She pointed.

"Finger bowls?"

Business-like, B.J. responded, "Yes."

The flight attendant looked at Mary Jean and me, one eyebrow raised slightly. "Did you want one too?" We shook our heads, me thinking that, as middle-aged women, we needed to accept our station in coach.

But not B.J.. Sinking her hands into the lemon water, she sighed slowly and deeply. She took the warm cloth from the bowl, squeezing water over one hand and then the other. After she'd wrung the cloth and patted her hands dry, she leaned back, closing her eyes blissfully. "I just had to ask. It's not like anyone owes me anything. I mean, we're going to M-E-X-I-C-O!"

Some part of me might have felt guilty for going to Mexico with my friends. But Theresa, the relationship therapist my husband and I went to, had absolved me of guilt. Together we had wrangled. I was unhappy paying rent for Doug's art studio when his art-teacher income didn't cover the rent. He didn't want me to leave him for 10 days with my friends while he bore responsibility for our teen daughters and our preteen son who had complex medical needs. So Theresa brokered a deal: She convinced us that Doug needed the studio and I needed the annual trip.

I knew B.J. and Mary Jean individually before they knew each other. First I met B.J., in a group of visual artists and writers coordinated by an inner-city church. Compact with broad, strong hands, B.J. had studied sculpture at university, worked for the school district and was a single mother to three school-age kids, their father bailing when the youngest was still in diapers. I loved B.J.'s passion for making art. I loved listening to her talk. Her small jaw and perfect white teeth formed definitive statements. Her hair managed to accentuate her chiseled face more elegantly the more unruly it got.

I met Mary Jean through a network of parents of kids with disabilities. She was in the process of moving from the condo where she raised her sons after her Fortune 500 husband took off, not supporting the boys at all during their school years. She planned to move to a year-round houseboat on the Mississippi in St. Paul.

"I'm a water person," she'd said.

"What about the long winters?"

"The boat gets iced in. I'll have a fireplace. Services from the dock stay hooked up."

"It's worth it to you, the winter inconveniences?"

"Oh yeah," she spoke decisively. "I know some marina live-aboards. Everybody gets by."

Mary Jean first taught elementary classes in grade school but moved on to coaching families of people with mental illness. She read the news on KFAI radio every Monday, in her beautiful speaking voice. Mary Jean's finely honed bullshit meter benefited me tremendously. I was the most gullible of the group, possibly a function of denial. I'd stayed in a narrow channel of social development, marrying at 19 and having kids in my 20s while going to a Catholic nursing school. Mary Jean was tall and carried herself with dignity. Her sculpted arms and tapered fingers accented her words. She'd grown up dancing, unlike B.J. and me, whose parents forbade dancing on religious grounds. Whenever I appeared skeptical at her enthusiastic praise for my contributions to the world, she'd say, authoritatively, "Trust me." I did trust her.

And I wondered: How had I gotten lucky enough to meet these two, to study them in a place like this, learning to emulate their remarkable strength?

We lounged on our twin beds in a spacious tiled room at Hotel Irma in Zihuatanejo, before finding a taqueria for dinner. Lying on her back, B.J. rested an ankle on the other bent knee. This was a working vacation for her, and she marshalled energy to make the most of her hunt for beautiful things to incorporate into her art. “I’m starting a list of supplies to make tourist art. I’ll use little talismans, gems, beads, milagros, bits of painted tin, whatever. Small 3D pieces that radiate a kind of promise, protection, blessing. For women especially.”

“A lot of people would love those.” Mary Jean sat upright, filing her nails.

B.J. continued. “I’ve seen art like that in Tucson but have something a little different in mind. If you want to help me sort through Milagros at the stalls, there are certain ones I’ll use. Arms, legs, hearts, breasts, hands, feet.”

Through doors flung open to palm trees rustling against the bluest sky beyond our terrace, birds squawked. Waves exploded on rocks far below us at the base of the bluff. Propped on an elbow, I stared into the tropical luxury, inhaling the scent of paradise.

“I’m up for that. Can’t be at the beach all the time!” I knew the sound of the waves would eventually obliterate the crisis loops in my head. I’d bodysurf. I’d find beautiful stones, shells and beach glass.

Mary Jean laid her file on the bedside table. “Me too. There’s room in my schedule.” She ticked off her list on opposite fingers as her green eyes gazed thoughtfully upward: “Water, sun, bougainvillea appreciation, paperbacks under a beach umbrella, wandering the shops, diving into local cuisine …”

Even when she wasn’t using her announcer voice, her delivery was sonorous, her promises solid.

TUESDAY WRITING CREW

By Katie Noah Gibson

Tuesday morning, 10:30 a.m. Eastern time. I log in to Zoom, hair still damp from my post-run shower, a swipe of eyeliner firmly in place. Nina, Tina and Debra have arrived ahead of me, trading stories about Nina's podcast and Debra's latest cooking adventure and the antics of Tina's senior dog, Gibson. I reach for my mug of tea as the others appear: Jody, Chris, Marsha, Leslie, Rachel, the other Leslie, Ruth Ann. We come from all over the country: Boston, Minneapolis, Utah, the Midwest. It's a writing class, but it's also a community—the one that ended up saving my life during the long months of the pandemic.

I'd known Nina online for years before COVID, through our blogs and Twitter and the overlapping of our mutual circles online. Sometime in the summer of 2020, one of her Instagram posts caught my eye. The writing classes she usually taught in person in Minneapolis had gone virtual and thus were open to anyone. I didn't hesitate. Furloughed from my job in communications at a college and living alone in a studio apartment, I was desperate for any form of connection and community. The writing—at least initially—was a bonus.

I had first-day jitters that September, of course, wondering how it would feel to walk (even virtually) into a roomful of total strangers. But I needn't have worried. The group members, both veterans and a couple of other newbies, put me immediately at ease. They were (and are) warm and friendly and intelligent, welcoming me as a comrade from the very start. We quickly developed inside jokes—teasing Nina about her "Ted Lasso" fandom, admiring the wall of meticulously color-coded Post-it notes behind Chris' desk, debating whether Rachel's New Jersey accent or the various Midwestern drawls were thicker. But we always eventually got down to the writing.

Each week, after everyone shared what they'd been up to creatively, Nina shared a writing prompt, read it aloud, and gave us 20 to 30 minutes to write on our own. After we came back together, everyone who wanted to would read her work aloud, as the others listened in and wrote cheering comments in the group chat: "Great details!" "Hilarious!" "Love that last line!"

Unlike some of the others, I was not (yet) working on a book or another substantial project. Sometimes those Tuesday scribbling sessions were the only "real" writing I got done during the week. I wrote countless drafts of essays processing my divorce, often silently weeping as Nina stepped in to read my words aloud to the group. I wrote about pandemic loneliness, about my relationship with my partner, about my regular runs through East Boston and the flowers and trees I saw each day. I was, in short, recording and sharing my life and listening as the others did the same. We made space for each other to share memories and longings, crisp details and complicated feelings, humorous incidents and life-altering pain or joy.

A year into the pandemic, we gathered in Minneapolis for a celebratory weekend. There was happy hour at Debra's, a big long-table dinner at a Mexican restaurant, smaller groups of us writing together or going to bookstores and talking as though we'd never stop. That weekend helped confirm for me that these women were not only writing partners, but friends.

We were married, single, partnered, divorced, mothers, pet parents, child-free. We were published, unpublished, never-want-to-be-published, publishers, podcasters, poets. We were stay-at-home moms, freelancers, accountants, retirees, lawyers, businesswomen. We were Christian, Jewish, late-in-life converts, nonreligious, refugees from the religious communities that once ruled our lives. We were runners and walkers, tennis players and reluctant exercisers. There was more diversity, more variety, in this group of women than one would ever imagine looking at us from the outside.

We shared it all on Tuesday mornings, knowing it wouldn't go any farther than our conversations and our computer screens. We trusted, exclaimed over, delighted in and encouraged one another. And then we'd wave goodbye until the next session, leaving (at least in my case) with buzzing brains and full hearts.

Now that our lives and the world are shifting, so is the group. I'm not sure what the future holds for this group, or my own place on the weekly Zoom calls. But for now, some of us still gather: to write, to laugh, to commiserate and share. We write to process, to celebrate, to try new things, to make sense of our experience in the world. We share our lives for a couple of hours every Tuesday. We are, though the particulars have shifted, a community. And we are better—always—together.

WHEN PREGNANCY DOESN'T GLOW

By Jillian Netherland

Two pink lines. The instructions indicated to wait up to three minutes for results, but mine showed immediately.

I was pregnant. I was finally going to be a mother.

It was a surreal and beautiful time of closeness with my husband, the two of us sharing this special secret; however, the moments of excitement were gone almost as quickly as they had arrived. Darkness unexpectedly crept in and consumed every thought and feeling I had.

What began as something I couldn't wait to celebrate became a source of shame and despair. I delayed announcing my pregnancy. I avoided discussing the baby. I did not create a registry or nest. Prenatal bonding felt foreign and impossible.

Recognizing that these feelings were not normal was easy to do; admitting that I was feeling them was not. Pregnancy is meant to be a time of joy. The fact that it was the opposite led me to believe something was severely damaged at my core, unfit and unworthy of becoming a mother. I didn't want anyone to see what I saw in myself during this time, so I hid it, hoping the "fake it 'til you make it" mantra would work, while I suffered privately in silence.

Our daughter was born full-term and perfectly healthy. The bonding came at once. I instantly fell in love with the tiny person who, despite everything I had felt leading up to her arrival, I had waited my entire life to meet.

In addition to this deep, pure love, I found myself weighed down by the heaviness of another intense feeling: guilt. How much of what I had experienced during pregnancy transmitted to her in the womb? To say it had not been a happy pregnancy was an understatement. She deserved better.

Halfway through our hospital stay, a nurse inquired how I was doing. For the first time, I admitted it all—the truth about my pregnancy and the fears I was now experiencing because of it. She listened, and when I finished, she told me about something I had never heard of—antepartum depression.

Like postpartum depression, antepartum depression is triggered by hormonal changes, except this version occurs during a person's pregnancy. Whether it is not as common or often left unaddressed, fewer cases of antepartum depression are documented, making it less known and less talked about.

I now had a name for what I had experienced and a reason behind it. It had nothing to do with who I was as a person; it was chemical.

Antepartum depression places those who experience it at higher risk for postpartum depression, so when we left the hospital as a new family of three, I was sent on my way with ample checklists to keep tabs on myself, as well as a packet of resources.

Among these was a meetup group for moms of newborns, held every Friday at the hospital.

Despite being an extrovert, I was hesitant. Stepping out of

the shadows of antepartum depression left me feeling robbed and behind the curve in motherhood; I was certain this group would only be another source of shame.

The days turned to weeks, then one month, then two. With my husband back at work, the strange sensation of new-parent isolation began to set in, and the mom group started to become more appealing.

I parked my car, fussed briefly with the baby carrier before opting for the stroller instead, and then crossed the parking lot to the hospital's double glass doors. The group was easy to identify: a dozen women with babies sitting in an oval adjacent to the main lobby. The facilitator greeted me with a warm smile and a hug before directing me toward two women who would soon become two of my closest friends. All previous concerns quickly dissipated as we shared who we were, talked about victories and challenges we were experiencing, and concluded with a delightful round of baby yoga. The hour flew by, and I found myself leaving with a fresh appreciation for my new season in life, counting the days until the next meetup.

In this space, I experienced friendships formed quickly due to common ground and a shared need for connection. Motherhood is a life-changing experience, one that can neither be understood nor truly prepared for until you are in it—and here we were, navigating this new normal together. I had found my healing village, and my daughter was part of it with me, forming her own early friendships.

Shortly after celebrating four months with our daughter, my husband and I learned I was six weeks pregnant with our second baby. Two children were part of the plan; having them this close together was not. With my first pregnancy and the hopelessness that accompanied it not far behind me, I was nervous—but this time was different. I knew now what to look for, and because my husband and new group of mom friends were aware, I was not going into this alone.

My second pregnancy was as full of light as my first was dark, allowing me to enjoy every milestone—internal and external—as it was happening. I was witnessing my daughter's firsts as a person while I was experiencing my own firsts as a parent right along with her, all the while growing her baby sister. I had the love of my husband, something that is irreplaceable and incomparable, but I also had the often unsung yet invaluable love and support of a group of women who were present for the purest reasons of all: they cared, they understood, and they wanted to be part of it.

A quote by an unknown author making its rounds through social media states, "Each time women gather in circles with one another, the world heals a little more." For me, this magic is undeniable—I witnessed it firsthand while sitting with other new mothers on a hospital floor.

WHEN THE WORLD SHUT DOWN

By Miranda Scotti

When the world shut down, we couldn't gather. From across the country to across the state to across the city to across the street, invisible barriers caged us inside, and it no longer mattered how close or far we were. For three weeks, everyone was the same distance from everyone else, which may as well have been across the universe. I felt scared and hopeless and so very alone, but no matter what, there was a constant stream of words finding their way to me from the women who held me up. Like the invisible string my mother once told me connects us all, we gathered in the only space we could, inside the tiny message boxes of our phone screens. Their words wrapped around me the way their arms could not. We wept, we laughed, and we grew stronger together, even when we felt like we were falling apart. Three weeks, it turned out, was only the beginning.

And our friend text thread looked something like this:

What is social distancing?

Where can I find toilet paper?

I've locked myself in the bathroom so
I can get just one minute alone.

I'm hiding from my sourdough starter.

Is there a shortage of sidewalk chalk?

Any book recs?

How did it go?

Spare no detail.

Should I get a houseplant?

Moving back to Florida.

I need more coffee.

I'm changing from my nighttime to my daytime pajamas.

Dinner ideas?

I heard he has COVID.

There are so many sirens.

Another pandemic dream.

I miss everything.

Please don't give up.

When will this end?

And when the lockdown was lifted for everyone else, I needed those texts to lift me up more than ever as new invisible lines were drawn. Essential workers headed back into the line of duty, where they would face total burnout behind their masks. The most vulnerable of the population stayed home, rusting indoors in a strange kind of collective solitude, alongside only those in our quarantine pods. It was like "Groundhog Day," but not. A new normal, but not normal at all. I learned the word "ableism" and felt it in my soul. Human connection became nearly impossible outside my own home. There was only one other place I could turn.

And our friend text thread looked something like this:

I'm still in pajamas.

I'm out of coffee.

Did you hear that new song?

Guess who started walking?!

I am so weary.

The tooth fairy is coming!

Up for a promotion.

Going to a funeral.

I need some pizza.

Afraid I have COVID.

Waiting for the doctor.

I miss you all.

We're almost 40!

Let's plan a trip.

I hope I can come.

Leaving a treat at your front door.

I'll wave from the window, but I will not unpajama.

Mental health check?

I'm not OK.

We love you.

It's OK to not be OK.

We're all just human.

Here when you need us.

This won't be forever.

And when the vaccines arrived, we were told only the immunocompromised had to worry anymore, but that included me and my unit. Another strain appeared, and the opposition began. Nowhere felt safe—not in real life, not on social media, not even in my own mind at times. It was too hard to watch the world go on, even though it seemed like maybe it was all burning out there. I couldn't go to the grocery store or the library or out for a little treat or even to the dentist. I still couldn't gather, but the messages continued, and I was never alone. Not really.

And our friend text thread looked something like this:

Remember that time ...

I don't want to be essential.

I need a new job.

I don't want to home-school.

I don't want to get sick.

Oh, BTW I'm pregnant.

I miss going to Target.

I can't hold it together.

Friend text threads aren't therapy,
only therapy is therapy.

Happy birthday!

Still in pajamas.

I'm back on Zoloft.

Election results!

Surgery date is set.

You've got to hear this podcast.

I miss your faces.

Please send some good memes.

Laughing my ass off.

We all got COVID.

20-year reunion?!

I finished my novel.

Going on a cruise.

I'm afraid that it's over.

Keep us updated.

This feels like forever.

And when it's safe enough, we'll gather again, for that 40-year trip we've been trying to plan for years. We'll rent a house on the coast in Miami and pretend we're the Golden Girls for a whole week. I'll be Rose and I'll get to wrap my arms around my Blanche and my Sophia and my Dorothy in real life. We'll gather in the living room and sit on palm-patterned sofas while wearing silky nightgowns. We'll chat in the living room and drink coffee in the kitchen. We'll forget to go eat out or go sightseeing or shopping. We'll do exactly what we did those first three weeks when the world shut down, and we'll do it together, but this time in person. When it gets late—which, let's face it, will probably be 10 p.m.—we'll go to our rooms and lie in creaky beds, our nightgowns scrunching up around our 40-year-old hips. We'll take out our phones and start tapping away.

And our friend text thread will look something like this:

Thank you for being my friends.

Your pals and confidants?

LMAO

Cheesecake for breakfast?

Is that even a question?

I always knew we were Golden.

We're so good at being old.

Case in point, I am still in pajamas.

This is the best week.

I wish it could last forever.

WOMEN'S NIGHT OUT

By Kara Douglass Thom

Pictures from near the beginning of time returned from the largest telescope ever built, orbiting some 1 million miles from Earth. I have difficulty staying present and also understanding time travel. Only recently I learned the phases of the moon. But doesn't everyone, intuitively at least, understand the law of attraction? Not to be confused with seeking approval. I learned this late, too. What does it mean to see the deep past then? How will this help us now? Light that is 13 billion years old looks like a view from my kaleidoscope in 1977. Exploding stars from primeval galaxies replicate the pattern on my bedspread in the early 1990s. Is anything what it seems? What you actually call it? What I know about how matter creates itself is 10 women gathered around a table; the heat of summer, oppression, inequality, producing a new cosmos, all while stars, light-years away, are forming and dying.

EDITORS AND CONTRIBUTORS

ANNA BEFORT, SENIOR EDITOR

As a writer, editor and yoga teacher, Anna believes strongly in the power of words to connect us. She is passionate about using that power to uplift women's voices and create spaces where women can connect to their own innate wisdom, creativity and wholeness. Her work in publishing has spanned two decades and included managing editor roles at Mpls.St.Paul Magazine and MNSights Magazine.

CHRIS OLSEN, EDITOR

Chris is the founder of Publish Her, a female-founded publishing company, and Publish Her Story, a storytelling platform and magazine dedicated to elevating the words, writing and stories of women. A broadcast media veteran turned communications consultant, educator and author of "Whyography: Building a Brand Fueled by Purpose," Chris has helped thousands of women tell their stories and publish their books. Since 2018, Publish Her has awarded more than $250,000 in grants and services to underrepresented business owners and authors.

WENDY ALTSCHULER, CONTRIBUTOR

Wendy is a Chicago-based travel writer and mother to three teenage boys. Her book, "Perfect Day Chicago," is great for locals who rarely venture out of the Loop as well as travelers visiting the city for the first time. Follow her on Instagram: @wendyaltschuler.

THE CEDAR RIDGE WRITERS, CONTRIBUTORS

The Cedar Ridge Writers group is comprised of Morgan Baker, Sara Dovre Wudali, Eileen Drennen, Heidi Fettig Parton, Nina Gaby, Shelley Hewins Brown, Amy Kimball, Cynthia Leiffer, Janice McCrum, JoJo Narigon, Kristen Paulson-Nguyen, Lisa Rizzo, Marian Rogers, Mary Thompson, Michele Vanstrom and Ryder S. Wyatt.

DEB DEBATES, CONTRIBUTOR

Deb lives in North Dakota with her husband, two children and one needy yet lovable black Labrador retriever mix. Her experience raising a son with autism and type 1 diabetes led her to start her blog, Micah and Me, to raise awareness and inspire others who are on a similar journey. www.micahandme.com

KARA DOUGLASS THOM, CONTRIBUTOR

Kara Douglass Thom's poetry has appeared in Lucky Jefferson, Sport Literate, The 2020 Texas Poetry Calendar and several online journals. She is the 2018 recipient of the Gaia Fenna Memorial Fellowship at Tofte Lake Center and a finalist for the 2019 Julia Darling Poetry Prize. She resides in Chaska, Minnesota.

KATHLEEN ENGLISH CADMUS, CONTRIBUTOR

Kathleen is a mother, grandmother, wife, writer and nurse practitioner. She holds a B.S. and M.S. from The Ohio State University and an MFA from Ashland University. Read more in her book, "Intertwined: A Mother's Memoir," and her essay "The Novice" in the anthology "Learning to Heal."

HEIDI FETTIG PARTON, CONTRIBUTOR

Heidi's writing has appeared in Brevity, Forge Literary, Fugue, Multiplicity Magazine, North Dakota Quarterly, River Teeth Journal's Beautiful Things, Sweet Lit, The Manifest-Station and more. Her Brevity essay "The Once Wife" was recently nominated for "The Best American Essays 2023."

KATIE HANUS, CONTRIBUTOR

Katie is an herbalist and lifelong learner on a quest to understand the world and humans around her. She is a blogger at The Nature Wheel, where she explores adventures with nature, food, ritual and ceremony.

KAROL JACKOWSKI, CONTRIBUTOR

Karol is on the faculty of Bay Path University's MFA in Creative Nonfiction. She has published several books, most recently "Sister Karol's Book of Spells, Blessings, and Folk Magic." Karol is a member of the Sisters for Christian Community.

AMANDA KENNEDY, CONTRIBUTOR

Amanda primarily writes creative nonfiction and memoir but has recently found joy in recycling life experiences and trauma into collages of fiction. She has excelled in avoiding writing for years by reading everything she could on writing, starting two writing groups, facilitating writing retreats, and even writing a writing group manual.

CINDY LEHEW-NEHRBASS, CONTRIBUTOR

Cindy is a Minnesota author, dance teacher, choreographer, health coach and mom of two young adults (one with special needs). She recently completed her MFA in poetry and creative nonfiction at the Rainier Writing Workshop. Her work can be found in multiple book anthologies and national newsletters.

MONICA LINDO, CONTRIBUTOR

Mónica has a passion for seeing new places, people and cultures. She taught literature and Spanish at public high schools in Connecticut and Washington, D.C., and TESOL in South Korea and Japan. She is currently working on a travel memoir about her experiences teaching in the U.S. and Asia.

J.J. MCGAWN, CONTRIBUTOR

J.J. is a former attorney who recently moved to the Twin Cities, Minnesota, where she spent many days as a child visiting her mother's family. She is married with two children and a rambunctious puppy.

JILLIAN NETHERLAND, CONTRIBUTOR

Jillian is a nonprofit fundraising professional and a writer at heart. A freelance editorial writer on the side, Jillian has a passion for poetry and has begun dabbling in short stories (both fiction and nonfiction) and essays. She aspires to publish a children's book inspired by her two daughters.

KATIE NOAH GIBSON, CONTRIBUTOR

Katie is a writer, runner, flower fiend, cyclist and Texas transplant based in Boston, Massachusetts. She does communications work for a small nonprofit by day and reads all the books by night. www.katieleigh.wordpress.com

KATHIE O'BRIEN, CONTRIBUTOR

Kathie O'Brien is a retired college professor and educational consultant turned writer. In 2019, her nonfiction story "It's Not Complicated" was a Kay Snow Writing Contest award winner sponsored by the Oregon Writers Colony. Her screenplay "One More Run" was produced by the Corvallis Film Lab in 2022.

SUZANNE O'BRIEN, CONTRIBUTOR

Suzanne writes about health, healing and the power of nature. Based in Minnesota, her writing has been published in the REI Co-op Journal, Dreamers Magazine, Adoptive Families, Literary Mama, Mutha Magazine and Months to Years. She is currently writing a memoir exploring her relationships with her daughter, mother and grandmother.

ANNE PINKERTON, CONTRIBUTOR

Anne is author of the memoir "Were You Close?: A Sister's Quest to Know the Brother She Lost." Her essays and poems have appeared in Hippocampus Magazine, Modern Loss, Ars Medica and the anthology "The Pandemic Midlife Crisis: Gen X Women on the Brink," among other publications.

JANE RAMSEYER MILLER, CONTRIBUTOR

Jane is a Minnesota-based singer, activist, composer and choral conductor. She works as artistic director for GALA Choruses, a network of around 200 LGBTQ+ choirs. She has degrees in music and psychology but credits her best training to growing up in a Mennonite community surrounded by a cappella singing.

JOY RIGGS, CONTRIBUTOR

Joy is author of the nonfiction book "Crackerjack Bands and Hometown Boosters: The Story of a Minnesota Music Man." Her essays have appeared in Hippocampus, The Manifest-Station, HerStry, Of Rust and Glass, BLUNTmoms and StarTribune. She lives and writes in Northfield, Minnesota. www.joyriggs.com

LINDSEY ROSE, CONTRIBUTOR

Based in Minneapolis, Minnesota, Lindsey is a mom, writer and longtime public relations professional. After recovering from colon cancer in 2012, she launched a communications consultancy that supports food and retail brands. She is a passionate autism awareness advocate, dog lover, yogi and cookie baking aficionado. Follow her on Instagram: @LindseyRosePR.

SARAH SCHELLENBERG, CONTRIBUTOR

Sarah is a single mom of three and a former educator. She's usually sweaty (not because she's fit, but because she's often anxious or having a hot flash) and might try to be a writer now.

MIRANDA SCOTTI, CONTRIBUTOR

Miranda is a lifelong writer and daydreamer. She works in a library to maximize her time spent drinking coffee while surrounded by books. Miranda has had stories published in two anthologies, as well as a short story published by Voyage YA. To Follow her on Instagram: @mirandasbooked.

JODY VALLEE SMITH, CONTRIBUTOR

Jody is a writer, children's book author and magic maker residing just outside of Minneapolis, Minnesota. Her storytelling is inspired by her teenage daughters, who navigate the world using their imagination, grit, smarts and whimsy. Jody believes compassion, humor and a little more play can change the world.

KRISTA WESTENDORP, CONTRIBUTOR

A former pediatric palliative care and hospice nurse, Krista's writing has appeared in The American Journal of Hospice and Palliative Medicine, The Linden Review and the Star Tribune. She's working on a memoir about raising her son, one of the first generation of children to survive and thrive because of advanced medical technology.

KRIS WOLL, CONTRIBUTOR

Kris is a Minneapolis, Minnesota-based writer and educator and mystic at heart. Her essays and stories on home, history, family and food have appeared in local and national publications, and she has shared her work on stage in four "Listen to Your Mother Twin Cities" live storytelling events.

www.ingramcontent.com/pod-product-compliance
Lightning Source LLC
Chambersburg PA
CBHW030610310726
48979CB00003B/649
9781962457002